"Praying with one's feet changes everything—not only religion and spirituality but also lives and communities, and even words spoken or written. Lindsey Krinks takes her readers on a journey in which this insight deepens on every page. She brings together the personal and the political, with a hint toward economic possibilities."

—**Joerg Rieger**, distinguished professor of theology, Cal Turner Chancellor's Chair in Wesleyan Studies, and director of the Wendland-Cook Program in Religion and Justice, Vanderbilt University Divinity School

"*Praying with Our Feet* reminds us that theology is meant to be lived out, not sequestered in the ivory towers of academia. This book shines a light on the people who need our solidarity more now than ever. Praise for Lindsey Krinks for writing such a timely read for all of us."

—**Robyn Henderson-Espinoza**, founder of the Activist Theology Project

"I wholeheartedly say amen to *Praying with Our Feet*. The continued growth of poverty and homelessness in the richest country in the world is a moral failing and a social sin. Those who have decided to devote their lives to the faithful and who struggle to uplift all of God's children, from 'the least of these' to 'all of these,' need to be heard. The story Krinks tells in her book is one of an important and needed ministry of work with the poor and homeless. It is a story among many other untold stories of unsung saints."

—**Willie Baptist**, activist, educator, author, and formerly homeless father

"Krinks reminds us time and again that one life does make a difference—be it our own or another's—and this is both gift and grace. Our world desperately needs not only our caring but also our actions to heal and to continue to point us to the new heaven and new earth where justice and love find their home. This is a powerful book of stories that will keep you reading."

—**Emilie M. Townes**, dean and distinguished professor
of womanist ethics and society, Vanderbilt University
Divinity School

"Activist, theologian, and sister in the struggle Lindsey Krinks weaves together stories from her upbringing with stories of those left out of the prosperity God intends for all. With great sensitivity and honesty, she calls people to fix their gaze on the stark reality of poverty and homelessness, and witnesses to how poor and homeless leaders and people of faith and conscience endeavor to do something about it. I am familiar with many of the people's stories lifted up by Krinks and thank her for treating the lives and wounds of so many of God's people as serious and sacred, and for recognizing them as moral and political agents of change."

—**Liz Theoharis**, cochair, Poor People's Campaign;
codirector, Kairos: The Center for Religions, Rights,
and Social Justice, Union Theological Seminary

PRAYING

with

OUR FEET

PURSUING JUSTICE AND HEALING
ON THE STREETS

LINDSEY KRINKS

Brazos Press

a division of Baker Publishing Group
Grand Rapids, Michigan

© 2021 by Lindsey Krinks

Published by Brazos Press
a division of Baker Publishing Group
PO Box 6287, Grand Rapids, MI 49516-6287
www.brazospress.com

Printed in the United States of America

Library of Congress Cataloging-in-Publication Data
Title: Praying with our feet : pursuing justice and healing on the streets / Lindsey
  Krinks.
Description: Grand Rapids, Michigan : Brazos, a division of Baker Publishing
  Group, [2021] | Includes bibliographical references.
Identifiers: LCCN 2020033028 | ISBN 9781587434587 (paperback) | ISBN
  9781587435287 (casebound)
Subjects: LCSH: Christianity and justice. | Church work with minorities. |
  Marginality, Social—Religious aspects—Christianity. | Civil rights—Religious
  aspects—Christianity. | Minorities—Civil rights—United States—History—20th
  century. | Prayer—Christianity.
Classification: LCC BR115.J8 K75 2021 | DDC 261.80973—dc23
LC record available at https://lccn.loc.gov/202003302

The author is represented by The Christopher Ferebee Agency, www.christopherfere
bee.com.

Some names and details have been changed to protect the privacy of the individuals
involved.

21   22   23   24   25   26   27   7   6   5   4   3   2   1

To Andrew, my love,
and to my friends on the streets,
the living and the dead

"For many of us the march from Selma to Montgomery was about protest and prayer. Legs are not lips and walking is not kneeling. And yet our legs uttered songs. Even without words, our march was worship. I felt my legs were praying."

—Rabbi Abraham Joshua Heschel (quoted in Rabbi Michael Shire, *The Jewish Prophet*)

CONTENTS

AUTHOR'S NOTE

WHEN I SET OUT to write this book, I realized there was simply no way to name all the people, organizations, and faith communities who were present and active in many of these stories. I'm mindful of the outreach workers, service providers, volunteers, and movement friends who played significant roles in the events herein but are not named. I remain deeply grateful to be accompanied by so many of them and to share this work, this life, and this calling with them. None of us can do this alone.

Nearly all the people who appear in these pages have given me permission to use their real names. The only exceptions are a few public figures and ministers who could be easily found through an online search and a handful of friends from the streets who I was not able to track down; I have changed their names to protect their privacy.

The events that unfold in this book are told with as much accuracy and adherence to history as I am able to recall. In order to write this book, I spent extensive time going through newspaper articles, recorded interviews, documentaries, blogs, and old journals. Any errors are my own.

A note about the title: I first came across the expression "praying with our feet" as a college student. I was captivated by the marches, sit-ins, freedom rides, and boycotts of the civil rights movement. While I was reading about the 1965 march from Selma to Montgomery, I stumbled upon Abraham Joshua Heschel, a Jewish mystic, philosopher, and scholar of the Hebrew prophets.

Heschel grew up in 1930s Poland, where several of his family members were killed by Nazis. After fleeing to New York in 1940, he connected the evil of anti-Semitism and the Holocaust in Europe with the evil of racism and segregation in the United States. Compelled by his faith, Heschel became involved in the struggle for civil rights, becoming a friend and confidant of the Rev. Dr. Martin Luther King Jr.

Marching alongside King, Heschel said he felt as if his legs were praying. Like other mystics, Heschel knew that prayer is more than a stationary act confined to the spiritual realm. Prayer moves. It reaches into the physical, material, economic, and political realms. It takes on flesh so that our beliefs become uttered "not only with our lips, but in our lives."[1]

Before being introduced to Heschel, I was familiar with other spiritual leaders who spoke of embodying their faith through action. The apostle James said, "I will show you my faith by my deeds" (James 2:18). Francis of Assisi is often attributed with saying, "Preach the gospel at all times. If necessary, use words." Teresa of Avila, a sixteenth-century Carmelite nun, is believed to have said, "Christ has no body now but yours. No hands, no feet on earth but yours." Buddhist monk Thich Nhat Hanh taught that walking meditations can move us into greater awareness of the interconnectedness of all things.

Less than a week before the contract for this book arrived in the mail, my husband, Andrew, and I attended the unveiling of two historical markers in Nashville to remember victims of lynching and racial terror. One of the speakers, a Black organizer with We Remember Nashville, recited an African proverb. "When you pray," she said, "move your feet." The next week, I learned that Frederick Douglass, a former slave, author, and nineteenth-century abolitionist, put it much the same way. "I prayed for twenty years," he is credited with saying, "but received no answer until I prayed with my legs."

As a white woman from the South wrestling with my own sense of place and calling, it was not until I encountered such mystics and freedom fighters—even those whose biographies and traditions differ fundamentally from my own—that I was able to find myself more fully, to grasp the connection between spirituality and activism, and to locate my story as a complex part of the broader, still-unfolding drama of faith and the struggle for justice.

By using "praying with our feet" as the title, I don't intend to imply that my life and the embodied prayers that comprise it are comparable to the lives and prayers of authors and activists like Heschel and Douglass, who resisted the horrors of white supremacy and other systemic injustices from which I have benefited. My sincerest hope is to channel the notion of "praying with our feet" from its multiple sources as an expression of honor and gratitude to those whose lived prayers have fanned the flames of love, solidarity, and resistance in me.

PROLOGUE

"The night will give you a horizon further than you can see."
—David Whyte, "Sweet Darkness"

MY DEAREST LOVE, in part, this book is the story I have been longing to tell. It's a tale of descent, of journeying to the underside of society, of finding and being found. It's a tale of learning to pray with our feet when our spirits were weary about the state of the world. But this is also the story I thought I'd never tell. A story about the jagged edges of myself I couldn't smooth away— about all I've hungered for these long years. It took me until now to realize that this story is, at its heart, a love story. Between you and me, yes. But so much more. It's a story of falling in love with a people, with a struggle, with this world and all its madness. It's the story of a seeker searching for belonging, for some spark, some horizon of hope.

My prayer for so long was that you wouldn't be singed by my fire, that at least you would come out of this unscathed. But you have been burned by my flames, cut by my edges. This book bears witness to our scars. The miracle is that we came into this together and that we're still standing. The miracle is that for every lick of flame that scorched us, we have been given a healing salve that only the wounded healer knows.

So come with me to the place it all started. Come with me to the streets where we pray with our tears, our hands, our fury, our feet. Come with me to those tender, fierce, hurting places where we find both our undoing and our salvation. Come with me into the night.

1

UPSTREAM

BE COOL, I told myself, wiping sweaty palms down the front of my jeans.

The student center ribbed around me like the empty belly of a whale. My nerves were coiled, my hands shaky. I felt like a wayward schoolgirl called to the principal's office—except it wasn't the principal's office. It was a "chat" with one of the top administrators of the university on an eggplant-colored couch, almost comfortable, beneath the buzz of fluorescent lights. I was, for the most part, a straight-A, straitlaced student. If I kept my head down, I'd walk across the stage, diploma in hand, in two months' time.

I sunk into the hot seat beside Andrew, a tall, lanky, bearded English major whose presence both calmed and kindled me. The administrator's mission? Reason with us. Set us back on the straight and narrow path that leads to order, success, salvation.

The administrator leaned toward us, elbows propped on his knees.

"You're too new to politics to understand that change doesn't happen through protests," he said, his saccharine tone sour.

3

Maybe he was right. I had organized volunteer projects before but had never been involved in anything like this. It was Nashville, Tennessee, 2007. Mayor Bill Purcell was drafting his last budget before leaving office. He had promised to build two hundred units of affordable housing, but the funding was missing from the budget. Without the money, his promise was hollow.

Homeless advocates and activists were beginning to apply public pressure. To support their advocacy, Andrew and I joined five other student organizers, including Richard, a chestnut-eyed sophomore who hailed from Huntsville and taught me how to smoke under Alabama skies. Our plan was to hold a letter-writing campaign on campus that would culminate in a march and rally at the end of the week to deliver the letters to Purcell. Despite collecting over seven hundred signed letters—well over our goal—the seven of us were still new to the intricacies of social activism. We still held the invincibility of youth, but as the week dragged on and tensions heightened, crescents of worry settled beneath our eyes.

As an outgoing mayor, what did Purcell have to lose?

Apparently, enough. Enough for someone in his office to call one of their friends who was a top administrator at Lipscomb University, our small, Christian liberal arts college. Enough for that administrator to summon us and recommend that we drop the action altogether and hold an educational forum on campus next fall.

"But the time to act is now," I countered, "*before* the budget address." Instead of sympathizing with our urgency, the administrator scolded us about how young, idealistic, and naive we were. He would later pull Andrew aside, man to man, hoping he could bring him to his senses. "I just talked to a very important person in this city," he told Andrew, "and the activists you're working with can't be trusted. Be careful who you associate with. You're both good students. I'd hate for anything to happen to you here."

My eyes stung. I felt certain we were doing a good thing—the *right* thing. But perhaps the administrator was right. We were certainly fresh. A heap of reasons we should cancel the rally, including the possibility of repercussions, weighed down our spirits. We left the student center feeling as if we were riding away on bikes with deflated tires.

We made our way to the computer lab where we still had hours of printing, planning, and emailing to do. In the lab, the minutes blurred into hours. My phone rang, a number I didn't recognize. The soft voice of a man on the other line said he was Father Charles Strobel. I combed my mind for a connection. *Father who?* He had heard about the rally and offered to give the opening prayer.

"Uhhh . . . ," I stammered. *Who was he again? How did he get my number?* "Would it be okay if I talk to the other students and call you back?" I asked.

I didn't know then that I was speaking to the former Catholic priest who was the father of homeless services in Nashville, founder of the nonprofit organization Room In The Inn, and the most trusted homeless advocate in the city—both on and off the streets. I also didn't know that I was speaking to the person who would become my mentor and close friend and who would walk alongside me as I cofounded another nonprofit and ripened into a homeless advocate, organizer, and chaplain myself.

Back in the computer lab, Andrew and I could barely keep our eyes open. Before we turned in for the night, we propped our backs against the wall in the hushed hallway. Andrew took my hand in his and tenderly cupped his other hand on top. Warmth entered my weariness. We closed our eyes and he prayed. He prayed that we would find discernment and courage, that we would be led where we needed to go. His words, his touch, opened a sea of calm in me that carried me all night long.

The next day, just three days before the march, Andrew's phone rang.

"This is Lieutenant Hawkins from central precinct. I understand you're having a march in a few days, and I see you don't have a permit."

I imagined Andrew's heart quickening. The lieutenant was right. This was our first march, and no one told us that we were supposed to request a permit *four* days before the event if we were expecting more than twenty people. We were expecting at least one hundred and were already past the deadline.

"I need you to give me your word that you won't march," he said. "If you march, you'll be putting yourself and your friends at risk of arrest."

Why did one of the top administrators at our school and a police lieutenant even care about this action?

What would happen if we defied them?

What would happen if we didn't?

Rip Currents

Rip currents act like rivers beneath the surface of the sea. Some nudge and tug, while others are powerful enough to sweep Olympic swimmers out beyond help. How do you survive a rip current? You swim at a beach with lifeguards. You learn to spot the signs. You train your eyes for the line of debris moving into the deep or for that eerie calm between breaking waves. You learn not to fight against the rip but to get out of the current altogether.

When I was growing up in South Carolina, my parents tried their best to protect me and my siblings from the rip currents of addiction and mental health problems that pulled several of our family members far from shore. I was in fourth grade when my Uncle Phillip ended his life, in sixth grade when my cousin Jonathan ended his. Other family members cycled on and off the streets, in and out of jails and treatment facilities. But I still recall, with cutting clarity, the day my Uncle Phillip was swept under.

My brother and I sat in silence at Nanny and Papa's kitchen table. Our parents were out of town. We had just gotten back from my cousin's baptism at church, and I was still wearing my black Mary Jane church shoes. A dozen burnt mozzarella sticks clung to a paper towel in a flattened wicker basket. We knew something was wrong. We ate slowly, keeping our eyes down. I wiped my greasy fingers on my dress beneath the table. The older family members talked in low, frantic voices. "Phillip's missing," we heard someone whisper. So they searched.

A small eternity later, Papa found Phillip's body and the gun in the attic of my cousin's house next door.

Why would God allow this to happen on the day his oldest daughter was baptized? What page in our family history had turned?

These questions haunted me. For years, I struggled to reconcile the cleaned-up version of my family with the distressed, dysfunctional version I saw from within. Later, I would learn about the festering wounds we covered, the smoldering secrets we carried. I would learn terms like "mental illness," "codependent," and "self-medicate." But as a child, I knew only how I felt in the face of such tragedy: powerless, uncomfortable, and confused.

Like a swimmer in fear of a rip current, I jumped out of the water altogether when I was eighteen. I left my home in the foothills of South Carolina, drove through the Smokies and Blue Ridge Mountains, across the Cumberland Plateau of Tennessee, and settled in the low roiling basin of Nashville. If I went far enough away, perhaps I could avoid the current that lapped at my feet. I poured myself into my studies in pursuit of a safe, comfortable, upwardly mobile life. Before I learned that my plans were not the sure and steady anchors I thought they were, I had a plan: I would finish my degree and become a physical therapist. I would marry a good Christian husband, have two to three kids, and land a well-paying job that would allow for a spacious house, a white picket fence, and plenty of vacation time.

It was comfortable for me to believe that poverty, homelessness, incarceration, and addiction were individual problems—isolated events that cursed my family or were caused by an accumulation of personal mistakes and character deficiencies. People who struggled and suffered made choices that led them down that path.

While I never said that aloud, I had absorbed those lessons from a society that worshiped individualism and a pull-yourself-up-by-your-bootstraps philosophy.

But sometimes the narratives that shore up our comfort begin to shift. Sometimes, when the wind is right, when we've stepped out beyond the walls that shelter us, greater truths stir us from our slumber and point our sails in a new direction.

I was first wrested awake from a third-row metal desk in a Biblical Ethics class the fall of my sophomore year. My professor, Dr. Lee Camp, was a master at waking people up. His Alabama-tinged voice resounded as he read statistics aloud: "Over twenty-nine thousand children under the age of five die every day from hunger and preventable diseases. While Americans spend eight billion dollars a year on cosmetics and Europeans spend eleven billion dollars on ice cream," he continued, "it would only cost six billion a year to provide basic education and nine billion to provide water and sanitation to over two billion people who live across the world without toilets, schools, and clean water." The statistics went on and on.[1]

As I drove home through Appalachia for Thanksgiving break my sophomore year, the statistics and numbers stayed with me. *Twenty-nine thousand* children a day. Twenty-nine thousand *children*. What did that number even look like? Did *they* do anything to deserve their lot? Where was God in that? If suffering was happening on such a large scale, why wasn't I doing more about it? I thought about my brand-name clothes, my make-up, my health insurance. I thought about the steaming food I piled on my plate every day, the bowls brimming with ice cream.

"It is important that awake people be awake," writes poet and conscientious objector William Stafford.[2] When I got home, I couldn't sleep. I felt suffocated by my own comfort and possessions. I felt choked by the food I wasted while others starved. I didn't know what to do, so I researched a nonprofit Dr. Camp had mentioned in class. They held an event called the 30 Hour Famine, during which students fasted to draw attention to global poverty and raise money to alleviate hunger.

After Thanksgiving, I brought the idea of hosting a campus-wide 30 Hour Famine to my girls' service club. They loved the idea, and we signed up to do the event the following February. We knew we had to do something to get people's attention, so we decided we'd cut out twenty-nine thousand paper dolls to hang up along the walls of the student center and dining hall. For six weeks, we spent every extra moment planning and snipping paper dolls out of old newspapers and magazines, handouts from recycling bins, and construction paper. Our fingers ached. We worked during class breaks. With bandage-speckled hands, we labeled baggies with the number of paper dolls each contained—fifty, one hundred, two hundred.

When we had twenty-nine thousand, or as close to it as our counting allowed, we took them to the student center late one Sunday night. An eerie quiet surrounded us. No one was in sight. We unraveled the chain of dolls from each bag and used several rolls of tape to connect them at the hands and hold them up. Beside the miniature assorted figures, we hung statistics and signs explaining what the paper dolls represented.

The next morning, nervous energy raced up my spine. When I got to the student center, the air was electric. A hush filled the space that once hummed with chatter. Students and faculty traced the lines of paper dolls upstairs to the dining hall and gathered around the signs and stats.

Flannery O'Connor wrote that when people aren't listening, you must sometimes shout, and when people aren't paying attention, "you draw large and startling figures."[3] So we did.

Some of the university administrators didn't appreciate our unconventional tactics. They had us remove the paper dolls the next week and created a policy that students had to get approval in order to post flyers in the student center. Despite the pushback, over one hundred students and a handful of faculty members participated in the first 30 Hour Famine.

9

Those who participate in the discipline of fasting know that something mystical can happen during a fast. You forgo something in the physical realm and set your gaze, your heart, your hunger on something beyond. "What eyes are for the outer world," says Gandhi, "fasts are for the inner."[4] The 30 Hour Famine was held during Lent, a season of fasting in the Christian tradition. One night, when I was at a contemplative Vespers service at Otter Creek Church, a passage from the book of Isaiah was highlighted:

> Is this the kind of fast I have chosen,
>> only a day for people to humble themselves?
> Is it only for bowing one's head like a reed
>> and for lying in sackcloth and ashes?
> Is that what you call a fast,
>> a day acceptable to the LORD?
>
> Is not this the kind of fasting I have chosen:
> to loose the chains of injustice
>> and untie the cords of the yoke,
> to set the oppressed free
>> and break every yoke?
> Is it not to share your food with the hungry
>> and to provide the poor wanderer with shelter—
> when you see the naked, to clothe them,
>> and not to turn away from your own flesh and blood?
>> (Isa. 58:5–7)

That passage burrowed in me like a seed in soil. I read the entire chapter again and again until it split, until it rooted, until it sprouted fiercely in my blood.

Modern-Day Prophets

Two years later, during my senior year, we launched Facing Hunger Week on campus with hopes of spurring action on issues of global and local poverty and hunger. The week would culminate with the third 30 Hour Famine. An international nonprofit would be our global partner, but we were still looking for a local partner to speak at an upcoming forum on campus.

One February afternoon, the air was unseasonably warm. Plagued with a case of senioritis, I skipped class with my friend Richard. We drove downtown to the Arcade, an old, open-air mall, to roam through free art galleries. We strolled through rooms of yellowing book pages cut and folded into art, enormous canvases sliced with flesh-colored paints, and exhibits of empty birdcages and mason jars containing specimens from everyday life. Hail the high art of young-adulthood angst.

As we wandered from gallery to gallery, I suddenly found myself in front of the wall-sized window of an office. Inside, statistics about poverty and black and white photos hung on every wall. The faces in the photos were weathered and worn but didn't shy away from the camera lens. I later learned that this was the photography of Tasha French Lemley, who was about to start *The Contributor*, Nashville's first street newspaper. The eyes that once looked straight into the shutter of Tasha's camera now pierced mine. The images held my gaze: winter trees and shanties cloistered in the shadows of an interstate overpass, a man sitting cross-armed with his bags beneath the concrete arch of a bridge, deep dirt creases like leaf-veins encircling the haunting eyes of a woman.

I stood there long enough for a woman to open the office door. "Uh, honey," she said with a hint of concern, "you wanna come in?" I nodded and stepped into the office of the Nashville Homeless Power Project—a group of people who were currently or formerly unhoused[5] and were organizing around issues of affordable housing, criminalization, and economic equity.

Inside, I met some of the lead organizers, including Bryan, then a resident at the Nashville Rescue Mission. Bryan waved me back to one of the filing cabinets. "I want to show you something," he said. He pulled out a newspaper clipping, a recent op-ed he had

11

written about the need for more affordable housing. Without hesitation, I invited a few of these organizers to speak at the forum. They agreed and we exchanged numbers.

A couple weeks later, Alonzo and Clemmie came to campus to represent the Power Project and talk to students about poverty and homelessness in Nashville. I got to the conference room early. Tasha brought photos to display and propped them on easels. Gradually, students and faculty began filing in, and before long, every seat was filled. We scavenged a few extra chairs from nearby rooms, but as the forum began, it was standing room only. There were over one hundred people packed in, with dozens of people lined against the walls.

"What are the causes of homelessness?" Alonzo asked. He stood, ignoring the seat provided for him. His dreadlocks were tied neatly behind his head, and his confident posture held everyone's gaze. "You've heard it said that people are homeless because they've got mental illness, because they want to be, because they're not trying." He continued, "But what we see on the outside are some of the *symptoms* of homelessness rather than the *causes*. They are the leaves of the tree. In order to understand what's really going on, we need to get down to the roots."

Clemmie, a former sex worker who would later be recognized as Nashvillian of the Year, picked up where Alonzo left off. "Look around at this city," she said. "The people on the streets aren't *home*less. They're *house*less. They're not lazy. They're working double shifts at jobs that don't pay the bills!"

"Right!" followed Alonzo. "You gotta understand that the root causes of homelessness are the lack of affordable housing and the lack of adequate wages. So why aren't our leaders doing anything about *that*?"

"It just so happens," said Clemmie, now also standing, "that good ole Mayor Bill Purcell has been making a lot of promises about making a dent in homelessness. He says we need to build two hundred units of affordable housing a year. Problem is, his last budget address is coming up, and guess what isn't in it?" She paused, placing her hands on the table. "Money for affordable housing!"

Students shook their heads in dismay. A larger understanding of what was going on was growing, and the frustration in the room was palpable. As I listened to Alonzo and Clemmie, my back propped against the wall, it was as if I was listening to the prophet Isaiah or Jeremiah. *Woe to those who make unjust laws and deprive the poor of justice* (cf. Isa. 10:2). *Woe to those who build their palaces by unrighteousness, their upper rooms by injustice. Woe to those who make their own people work for nothing, not paying them for their labor* (cf. Jer. 22:13).

> *"The people on the streets aren't homeless. They're houseless. They're not lazy. They're working double shifts at jobs that don't pay the bills!"*
> —Clemmie Greenlee

Alonzo and Clemmie knew homelessness inside and out. They knew the people, the institutions, the powers. They had descended into the living hell of our city's streets and jails and now bore witness to their experiences. They took us by the hand and pointed out the realities and injustices we had not yet learned to discern. *Here are city leaders who say what people want to hear but don't follow through. Here are the subhuman conditions people in our own city are living in—tents and alleys for homes, no food to feed their children.*

That night, my mind rolled over Alonzo's and Clemmie's words, the lives of the prophets we were reading about in class, and a well-known parable. In the parable, a villager comes upon a river where a baby is flailing in the water, rushing downstream. The villager jumps in, manages to pull the baby out, and then realizes another is coming. She jumps back in and rescues that baby too, only to see another barreling downstream. One of her friends runs to the village to get more help, and they soon set up a system for rescuing the babies, even establishing an orphanage in town. But the babies just keep coming, day after day. After nearly a week, everyone is exhausted. The first villager slumps on the riverside, utterly spent, until a revelation ripples through her head and heart. If she wants to change things, she can't stay in the village or at the riverside. She needs to journey upstream to find out why so many babies are being swept downstream in the first place.

All the volunteer projects I had organized and participated in up to this point had been downstream. If things were going to change, I would have to learn to journey upstream. The more I thought about the parable, however, the more I realized the idea of babies in need of rescue was problematic. By nature, babies are helpless, needy, dependent. They are incapable of their own agency, not yet able to speak. Bryan, Alonzo, and Clemmie, however, weren't needy, voiceless, or powerless. Perhaps those in the parable who were coming downstream—like people on the streets today—had experience and knowledge that the villagers—folks like me—did not have. Perhaps they had the ability to teach us about the terrain the river covers, its currents, and maybe even its source.

I was learning that I wasn't called to merely pray for city leaders to do the right thing. I was also called to act in tangible ways.

Through my friendship with members of the Power Project, I was the learner—not the rescuer. Some had been organizing for their rights since before I was born. They were teaching me that I could not ultimately address homelessness and other injustices through charity, service, and volunteerism alone. It would have to involve addressing what was upstream.

I was learning that I wasn't called to merely pray for city leaders to do the right thing. I was also called to act in tangible ways. "Suppose a brother or a sister is without clothes and daily food," says the apostle James. "If one of you says to them, 'Go in peace; keep warm and well fed,' but does nothing about their physical needs, what good is it? In the same way, faith by itself, if it is not accompanied by action, is dead" (James 2:15–17). I knew the passion I felt had to be channeled into concrete action in the world.

A couple days later, I called my new friends at the Power Project. "I've been thinking," I said. "What if we got students on campus to do a letter-writing campaign petitioning Mayor Purcell to include more money for housing in his final budget?" They were all ears. "And maybe then," I said, "we could have some sort of march or rally and deliver the letters?"

They loved that students were organizing and offered to support us however they could. The idea was born and we got busy.

Decision Time

Darkness pooled like water in the shadows as I slogged across campus for a meeting with the other student organizers. It was two days before the march and rally, and we were stuck between the excitement of those cheering us on and mounting pressure to cancel. As I slogged, the air smelled of leftover rain. Part of me pined for risk, the other sought stability. I prayed for a bolt of lightning to sizzle from the sky and strike true—to smite the path I shouldn't go. I prayed for some magic to weave together my fraying threads of certainty, to make me feel confident and whole. But no lightning sizzled, no grand tapestry of answers appeared. Instead, my face flushed against the cool of the evening.

We needed sound advice. Someone we could trust. And then, it hit me.

Father Strobel.

As it turns out, Father Strobel, whom I would later come to know as Charlie, had gotten my number from a friend at the Power Project. After realizing who he was, I called him back to accept his offer to lead the opening prayer. He was excited to hear that students were mobilizing and offered to help in any way he could.

15

And now, we needed that help. I updated him on our predicament and asked if he could meet us on campus.

The seven of us who were planning the action gathered in a small meeting room in a dorm on campus. Richard and Andrew opened a box of donuts and the sugary smell wafted through the room. Charlie walked into the lobby of the dorm wearing a heather-gray sweatshirt and matching sweatpants. If I told him now that I thought of him as a saint in sweats, he would wince with bashfulness. Charlie was in his sixties and had thin whitish-gray hair, eyes the color of far-off mountains, and a gentle demeanor. His presence alone brought a steadiness to the room. We told him about the tensions we were facing. Rather than telling us what to do, Charlie leaned in and asked, "Where are each of you in Scripture right now?"

Silence held. Gradually, each voice filled the void.

Isaiah.

Jeremiah.

The Sermon on the Mount.

Matthew 25.

The early church.

All of us were drawn to places of hope, places of resistance, places that turned society's rules and the status quo upside down. The poor were blessed, the hungry were fed, the wanderer was sheltered, and people were called to embody a kind of disruptive love in their actions.

When we brought up the opposition from authority figures, Charlie told us stories about his involvement in student protests in the 1960s. "You do realize that you have the authority to follow through with this action," he said. "That authority comes from the Spirit and from Scripture. It is the authority that has been lived out across time and is still being lived out in people like you today." He could tell we were still uncertain and afraid. "Here's the thing," he continued with a slight smile. "When you pray for patience, God will often give you difficult and trying circumstances so that you are forced to learn patience. Likewise, in order to become courageous, you must go through some frightening and challenging things." He paused and we leaned in. "Courage is not experienced in your heart until you face fear."

Charlie said goodbye a little before midnight. The seven of us huddled together when he left. We decided that we would continue with the rally, but instead of marching, we would simply gather on the lawn in front of city hall. We were young and not quite ready to test the police lieutenant's threat of arrest. But that would be the last time we ever let the police dictate whether we would march.

Turning the Page

The day of the rally had finally come. The sun held high in the cloudless azure sky, radiating the warmth of early spring. Richard, Andrew, the other student organizers, and I all wore red bandanas tied around our arms and foreheads. The Romanesque columns of city hall towered before us as we walked across the lawn. Already, dozens of people had gathered, carrying signs that read "Housing Is a Human Right" and "Ensure Justice."

I found Clemmie and she wrapped me in a tight hug. I stuttered through news interviews with her, and as the time to begin drew near, approximately two hundred people were there—students, professors, members of the Power Project, people on the streets, and other advocates.

The people who gathered formed a long line that snaked around the stairs of city hall. We handed a few letters to each person, and they delivered them one by one to the mayor's representative at the top of the steps. While the line moved forward, the crowd sang songs that Bryan passed out on sheets of paper. He had rewritten civil rights songs, changing tunes like "Will the Circle Be Unbroken?" to "Will the Cycle Be Unbroken?"

I stood to the side of the crowd as the songs echoed across the lawn, preparing to give the keynote address. I had my notes prepared but couldn't keep my hands from shaking and my voice from catching in my throat.

All my life, I had been conditioned by my upbringing in the Church of Christ to stay quiet. In that tradition, I was taught that God spoke through men—not women. When I asked why, my Bible school teachers quoted verses like 1 Corinthians 14:34 that said, "Women should remain silent." Ever since then, every time I tried to speak in public, my mouth felt stuffed with cotton. I had internalized the message that I shouldn't speak up. Despite feeling called to leadership roles, I had not received the practice or the encouragement that my male counterparts from the Churches of Christ had been given.

Before we started, Charlie walked over to me. "Looks like a pretty good crowd!" he said, his eyes lighting up with his smile. "How are you feeling?"

"I'm so nervous," I told him as my stomach knotted into itself.

"Would it be okay if I prayed for you?" Charlie asked. I nodded. He placed his right hand on my shoulder and began to pray over me. I closed my eyes. Sunlight poured over us. Time stretched and slowed. A new kind of breath filled my lungs. The words Charlie said to us Wednesday night came back to me: *You do realize that you have the authority to follow through with this action.*

When my eyes opened, my gait and hands were steady, my heart calm.

Charlie walked before the crowd. "In all my thirty years working on the streets," he said, "I've never seen a group of students gather like this."

Everyone erupted in applause. When the cheering died down, he led the opening prayer. After the "amen," stillness descended, and he turned to me and stepped aside. I felt my feet carry me out in front of my peers. I introduced the other student organizers and gave a shout-out to the Power Project. The crowd broke into applause. My hands, somehow composed, unfolded my notes.

"Today is a beginning," I started. "Today we hope to spark a community-wide movement. Today we hope to open a discussion that seeks creative ways to face the problem of homelessness in Nashville. We assemble out of a deep care and concern for our unhoused friends, and out of a great disturbance that our cars and pets receive more housing than our neighbors."

Members from the Power Project clapped and hooted as someone shouted, "Amen!"

"As students, we confess that we have not made addressing homelessness a priority in the past. But today, we commit to doing so in the future. We would also like to apologize to those who are unhoused, that we have accepted this injustice and that we have taken so long to speak out." I invoked the words of Clemmie and Alonzo, proclaiming that one of the root causes of homelessness was the lack of affordable housing. "We are here to ask Mayor Purcell to make housing a priority in his final budget proposal because we believe that housing is more than a need. Today, we declare that we believe housing is a condition of life, a human right."

Applause flared out again from the crowd. I called on the God of compassion and justice to be present and to spark change within us and our community. After I spoke, Andrew came forward to lead a closing prayer and we all joined hands, connected as never before.

March 2007 was a crucial time in Nashville's history. Later that month, a dozen housing advocates, including members of the Power Project and Charlie, would be arrested for civil disobedience on that lawn. A new mayor—Karl Dean—would be voted in that fall. New luxury condos were going up, with more in the planning stages. We could feel the social, economic, and political tides around us turning, but we didn't yet know how powerful their undertow would be.

As the rally ended, a euphoria danced in my bones. For once in my life, I was exactly where I was supposed to be. A man with a ruddy face and gray curly hair pushed his red-framed bike toward me across the lawn. I would later find out that he was a well-known advocate living on the streets and that he once ran for city council and knew the inner workings of our city government and our housing authority better than anyone. We would work together for years to come.

His eyes traced the front of city hall and the remnants of the crowd.

"Do you know what this means?" he asked. I shook my head. "You're an activist now," he said with certainty.

I searched his eyes with mine, waiting for him to break into laughter, say it was a joke, or tell me what I should do next. But his gaze held. My page had turned.

After the crowd dispersed, I walked across the lawn to a fountain with Andrew, Richard, and a couple other student organizers. Streams of cool water shot up from slick granite tiles, cresting high above our heads. We kicked off our shoes and ran beneath the fountain's spray. The water fell on us like pelting rain. I held my palm over a jet and it rushed out around me. Light and shadows cut through the spray, flashing around us.

I looked across at Andrew to see that he was also looking at me. Perhaps it was our late nights in the computer lab or our lengthy debriefing sessions after talking to administrators and authorities, but a kind of chemistry was growing between us. Without him, the rally would never have happened. Without him, I would have caved from the pressure or burned out altogether. Without him, I would have been a flame without fuel. I smiled, nearly blushing, and looked away.

Utterly drenched, we laughed our way to a patch of grass and dried out in the sun. We were exhausted yet invigorated. Blades of green rose up around our bare feet and arms. The cherry trees surrounding us were pink with bloom. More tensions and uncertainty would come down the road, but for the moment, we basked in the late afternoon light, washed and changed.

2

DESCENT

EVERY CITY has an underside. For every luxury condo and its gleaming rooftop pool there is a slum teeming with untended wounds, the stench and rot of decay, bedbug bites on the bellies of babes. Every city has a darker version of history told—or not told—by the conquered, the displaced. And as soon as I saw the first flicker of this wretched, blessed dark, I was drawn to the shadows like Icarus to the sun.

The first time I fell in love with the underside of a city was with Richard in 2006, a year before my baptism into activism. My heart hammered in my chest as I kept watch on Seventh Avenue to make sure no one was coming. Nightfall wrapped the buildings in deepening blues as what was left of the afternoon's rain shimmered on the pavement, holding a blur of golden lights. Richard lifted the heavy steel grate from the sidewalk and waved for me to climb in first, to descend beneath the city's surface on a cold iron ladder.

"Are you sure you've done this before?" I asked.

"Of course," he said with a grin, chestnut eyes glinting against the night.

Richard had a beatnik feel to him, with a tinge of magnetic grunge. Something reckless flickered in us both. He was careless and free in a way that drew me in, so down I climbed. My arms and legs quivered with adrenaline as I fumbled down each narrow rung. Richard followed me, closing the grate over our heads. I looked up from the bottom and could see slices of the world I knew above us. I was shaking but played it cool.

My eyes adjusted to the dim light of a round, concrete tunnel that smelled of metal and rust and grime. Two massive charcoal pipes ran alongside us, one to our left, one to our right. One carried cold water, the other hissed with hot. They traveled straight down Seventh Avenue as far as the eye could see, shrinking to a pinpoint in the distance.

"Ready?" he asked.

I must have nodded because we started walking along the damp, forbidden path between the pipes. We came across a blue-jean shirt crumpled in the shadows.

"Was that there the last time you came down here?" I asked.

Richard lowered his voice. "I don't know," he said, leaning in with a dramatic pause. "Maybe, if we're lucky, we'll both make it out alive."

"Not funny!" I said, shoving his shoulder.

I followed Richard, putting one unsteady foot in front of the other. We walked south, following Seventh, and turned left at the tunnel that ran beneath Broadway. Music from honky-tonk bars intermingled with the hiss of pipes. There was laughter. The sour tang of beer. A loudening cacophony of country music. Neon lights glimmering through grates.

This was our city, the city we loved. We had both walked up and down Broadway before; now we were beneath her shine. Later I would come to know the underpasses and alleys, the shantytowns and slums. I would learn that once you begin to notice the flattened cardboard and blankets beneath bridges, the footpaths into the woods behind gas stations, the flash of blue tarps through the trees, you never see things the same way again. Once you begin to understand the city not from above but from below, it changes everything.

Mind the Gap

The second time I fell in love with the underside of a city I was over four thousand miles away from Nashville. It was in 2007, a year after my walk below the streets with Richard. There were clouds laden with rain. The umber, roiling bend of the Thames. Cobblestone. Graffiti-stenciled concrete. Pubs. The smell of scones and smog.

A month after I walked across the stage in my cap and gown, I was on my way to London to complete an internship—my last college requirement. I said goodbye to Andrew, Richard, and my other friends—"we'll write," we promised—and flew across the Atlantic with several other students. The shadow of our plane raced the sun-drenched dawn, sweeping over cuts of English countryside. The sheep-speckled land gave way to cemeteries and steeples as we descended into the stone-hued city where we'd spend the next six weeks.

Our simple residence hall was located in the heart of Chelsea, one of the wealthiest neighborhoods in southwest London. Since the seventeenth century, Chelsea had been a haven of affluence, with the palaces of the ruling class dotting the landscape like cherries on a tart. Now, it was a high-end shopping mecca, home to celebrities and Mercedes dealerships.

My internship was in Central London, near the Houses of Parliament, where I was working with a group of advocates lobbying for the rights of local governments across the United Kingdom. My coworkers used words like "brilliant," "cheers," and "loo" that sounded novel to my American ears. We had at least three tea breaks a day and ate "biscuits"—American cookies—like it was nobody's business.

Before I left the residence hall on my first day of work, I tapped two pain relief capsules into my palm and swallowed them with a swish of water. My right ankle was already stiff and sore. Two years before, an indoor rock-climbing injury had left me unable to walk without aid for over a year. Despite an invasive surgery and months of therapy, my ankle still hadn't fully healed. Worry rose in my chest and troubled the flurry of excitement I felt. Working abroad would require walking and using public transit every day. Had I given this enough thought before coming?

It was only my first day and already I was running late. I hurried off the number 11 bus and headed toward the entrance of Sloane Square Station. Morning commuters wrapped themselves tight in fitted jackets and trendy scarves against the unseasonably cool air. They were sophisticated, confident, city-sleek, as if they were walking off the page of a magazine. And then I saw him. Worn, camel-colored coat. The weathered, soot-covered skin of a miner. He sat cross-legged on several sheets of newspaper in front of the station's entrance. He held out a plastic cup to collect spare change and looked ahead with dark, vacant eyes. As I stared at him, my mouth slightly agape, he turned his head and his distant gaze landed on me. His eyes met mine. My face flushed with recognition and guilt. My lips closed and tightened awkwardly.

My mind blanked. *What should I do? Come on, do something!*

A woman in a pencil skirt and blazer brushed past me.

You're already late, said a voice within. *Go.*

I turned away from the man and made my way to the Tube.

That weekend, I broke off from the group to explore the city on my own. I packed an extra bag of food in case I saw the man in the camel-colored coat. I was haunted by the way I shunned him, and while I knew I couldn't give him the keys to a new home, I could be kind. I could connect, affirm his humanity, exchange names, offer whatever I could. I stuffed a deflated rubber icepack into my bag beside the extra food. Taking medication at regular intervals wasn't enough to ease the soreness and pain in my ankle

24

from all my walking. As each day wore on, warmth gathered and pulsed across the joint, and the muscles along my arch tightened and strained. Rest. Elevation. Icing. Stretching. That is how I got through. That and reading. Nestled beside the food and icepack was Dorothy Day's autobiography, *The Long Loneliness*.

I first heard of Day in *The Irresistible Revolution* by Christian activist Shane Claiborne. Day was a bohemian journalist who converted to Catholicism and became an activist, anarchist, and pacifist. During the Great Depression she cofounded the *Catholic Worker* newspaper in New York. This was followed by the establishment of the Catholic Worker Movement, which was committed to serving those on the margins of society. Driven by the vision of creating a new world in the shell of the old, she lived in voluntary poverty, was arrested multiple times for civil disobedience, and started houses of hospitality and farming communities.

I ran my fingers across the soft white fray of the secondhand binding. Across the cover was a black and white photo of Day in her old age walking through winter woods. Half-moons of flesh hung beneath downcast eyes. Her hands were tucked into the pockets of her long overcoat, her back bent slightly forward, heavy from years of struggle and resistance. "Why was so much done in remedying social evils instead of avoiding them in the first place?" asked Day. "Where were the saints to try to change the social order, not just to minister to the slaves but to do away with slavery?"[1]

Her words burned in me as I turned the pages. I didn't realize how much I needed her analysis and example. I didn't realize then how much of my life she would change. I got off the number 11 near Sloane Square Station, but the man in the camel-colored coat wasn't there. As I boarded the Circle Line with the Tube map in one hand and Day in the other, I vowed to never make the same mistake—though I would again and again.

As I explored London and read Day, a burgeoning affection grew in me for the city and "the masses," as Day called them— the working poor who carry history and human progress on their backs and either are crushed beneath the weight or rise up to fight back. I came from a small town in the foothills of South Carolina and knew how to love the creeks and woods. I knew how to flip over river rocks and find salamanders and crawdads. I knew where wild mint and muscadines grew. But the city was a different animal altogether. Gothic architecture rose through the fog and hooves clopped on cobblestone. I rode red double-decker buses and then descended hundreds of feet below the city to board the Tube with untold thousands. During rush hour, I welcomed the crowds, the clutter, the chaos, the lights of the tunnel blinking and blurring through windows. I welcomed the closeness of bodies swaying in unison, pressing in at all sides.

As my love for the city grew, I became uncomfortable in Chelsea's easy comfort, and questions took root in me. Where should I go to find God? The church or the world? The spires or the streets? To what life was I being called? To one of comfort and upward mobility? Or to what Day called "the downward path that leads to salvation"?[2] My world was upside down. It seemed that those in power cared only about maintaining their power—power that insulated them from suffering. They hadn't learned to see the city from below. They were so high up they couldn't see the people being crushed. Why were a few people so powerful and wealthy while so many others were barely scraping by?

In the fourth century, just as Christianity was about to become the state religion of the Roman Empire, Basil of Caesarea said, "The bread in your cupboard belongs to the hungry; the coat hanging unused in your closet belongs to those who need it; the shoes rotting in your closet to the one who has no shoes. The money which you hoard up belongs to the poor."[3]

For me, Day was a twentieth-century manifestation of Basil's warning to the wealthy. "I did not see anyone taking off his coat and giving it to the poor,"[4] Day wrote. If we had extra coats, they belonged to the poor. If people around us were suffering, we had a responsibility to respond—not just individually but collectively.

Were unjust wars going on? We must resist them. Were people wasting away in the living hell of poverty and prisons? We must go to them. Day took this a step further. "Going around and seeing such sights is not enough," she insisted. "To help the organizers, to give what you have for relief, to pledge yourself to voluntary poverty for life so that you can share with your brothers is not enough. One must live with them, share with them their sufferings too. Give up one's privacy, and mental and spiritual comforts as well as physical. . . . Going to the people is the purest and best act in the Christian tradition."[5]

Reading *The Long Loneliness* was dangerous because of the truth that rose from the musty, yellowed pages. It was dangerous because of the questions it conjured, because of the power that came from a life lived in such generous abandon. What would it be like to know a city as intimately as Day knew New York and its masses? What would happen if I—if *we*—had the courage to live as if our deepest convictions were really true?

What would happen if I—if we—had the courage to live as if our deepest convictions were really true?

As I headed back to the dorm, I leaned my head back against the seat and closed my eyes. The chatter and whir of the bus grew distant, and my attention turned from Day to the hot, acute pain that engulfed my ankle. The throbbing of my ankle echoed through me, attaching itself to every heartbeat.

Two years before, when I was a sophomore in college and thought I had my future mapped out, I was at a rock-climbing gym. It was a cool Saturday morning in March. The air was fresh with spring and climbing chalk. I spent so much time at the gym that I had developed thick calluses along the meaty parts of my fingers and palms. As I was bouldering on the rock wall, adrenaline pulsed through me. For the first time, I was nearing the top. The muscles in my forearms strained, tight as rubber bands stretched to their limit. My fingers reached toward a crescent-shaped hold. I nearly grabbed it but couldn't secure my grip. Gravity took over and my body plummeted down. Instead of landing upright on the mat meant to break my fall, my right foot slipped off the edge and landed on the concrete floor, taking the full impact of my weight. A loud pop echoed through the gym while a burning sensation raced up my leg. In seconds, my right ankle ballooned to three times its normal size.

An X-ray revealed no broken bones. "You're lucky," said the doctor, "but you do have a third-degree high ankle sprain. You'll have to stay off your foot for the next six to eight weeks." I was given a large black boot to wear that strapped on to my foot and leg.

Eight weeks later nothing had changed. A second doctor recommended a cast for another six to eight weeks. His assistant wrapped my foot, ankle, and calf like a mummy, the wet plaster strips building and hardening with every layer. The cast was topped off with lime green.

After another eight weeks, it was time to start the fall semester and my ankle still hadn't healed. The muscles in my right leg were atrophied, and there was very little movement in my ankle joint. An MRI revealed everything the X-ray had missed. "It would've been better if you had simply broken the bone," the third doctor told me. "The internal damage is extensive."

That fall, I underwent my first invasive surgery. Bones were drilled, cartilage and scar tissue were scraped. I returned to my second-story dorm room confined to crutches. My rock-climbing calluses had softened and new blisters and calluses from the crutches spread across the top of my palms like tiny hardened hills. For months, I was completely dependent on others. I couldn't drive, go to the grocery store alone, or even carry my own food tray in the dining hall. I was on crutches for so long that other students started referring to me as "that girl on crutches," while some of the cute boys from my former days of ultimate frisbee started calling me Crutchy.

Some days, I was so weak I couldn't make it up the stairs to my dorm room. My friends folded themselves under my arms and carried me up like a battered doll. They left bright notes under my door that beamed with lines from the psalms. They refrained from sentimental quips like, "God has a purpose for your pain," which was not at all what I needed to hear. Instead, they rubbed my back at night while I melted into sobs of anger and frustration.

How many hours, days, and weeks did I spend in tears, watching the muscles in my right leg wither? It would be a year before I could walk without aid, and in that time, the comfortable life I was constructing would crumble like dry Carolina clay in my hands. I went into that gym convinced I would become a physical therapist and lead a safe, cookie-cutter life. I came out of that gym needing physical therapy and on the brink of a "dark night of the soul" experience during which I became well acquainted with my own suffering and the suffering of others and completely reexamined my vocational aspirations.

Honey and Night

Back at the residence hall in London, my friend Lauren poured a smuggled Cabernet into porcelain coffee mugs. The wine warmed me, eased my anxiety about my ankle. Lauren, an auburn-haired English major from Oklahoma, loved poetry and was unassumingly radical. We didn't know it then, but years later we would be arrested together, and she would become my closest friend. On our occasional nights in, several of us would gather in the common room to plan what parks to explore and what plays to attend. The wine we sipped was a small act of rebellion. Our study abroad program strictly prohibited drinking, even though we were within the legal drinking age. The documents we signed before coming on the trip made it clear that we could be sent home if we were caught. The mugs, we decided, offered a small measure of protection. It was a risk we were willing to take. And these days, I was more and more drawn to risk.

Before I left Nashville, Richard made me a "London Survival Guide" to accompany the mixed CDs he burned. In the guide, artwork and quotes from Banksy, the anonymous British street artist, flanked Richard's loving advice to me for the summer. "Flirt with one of the royal guards at Buckingham Palace in hopes of getting him to crack," he wrote. "If this is not accomplished, we will have a seriously strained relationship."

One of the Banksy quotes that Richard included read, "The greatest crimes in the world are not committed by people breaking the rules but by people following the rules. It's people who follow orders that drop bombs and massacre villages."[6] Our experiences with the rally several months before and our exposure to radical artwork, films, and literature were teaching us to question authority and reexamine what rules we chose to follow and why.

While we drank and discussed our days, I iced my ankle and massaged my foot. I had developed plantar fasciitis from all the walking, which meant that beads of knotted tissue ran along my arch. My only relief came from rubbing out the knots and icing my foot and ankle daily. The problem was that after several minutes of massaging, my fingers and thumb became so sore that I couldn't maintain the pressure. Lauren and others took my heel tenderly in their hands and worked the clumps of hardened tissue until they began to dissolve.

When darkness masked the manicured streets of Chelsea, I made my way to Picasso's Coffee Bar, the only nearby café open after five. The first time I ordered at Picasso's, the owner, a handsome middle-aged Middle Eastern man, told me that a cup of coffee would cost "twenty-five U.S. dollars." It wasn't until I saw his son's face break into a smile behind him that I realized he was joking.

I settled into a cluster of metal tables and chairs outside the café and time slipped away. At some point, the owner's son, who appeared to be about my age, came out to see if I needed anything. He offered me leftover baklava and I accepted. The flaky honey-layered pieces melted in my mouth while I savored them in pure pleasure.

"What are you reading?" he asked, leaning down. His dark features, the sharp curve of his nose, and his distinct profile all reminded me of Andrew. He too had eyes that drew me in.

"T. S. Eliot and an American beat poet named Lawrence Ferlinghetti," I replied, almost blushing. I pointed to *A Coney Island of the Mind* and he picked it up, gently thumbing through the pages.

After he went back inside, I closed the book and breathed in the smell of honey and night. I pulled out an unopened envelope from my purse—Andrew's most recent letter that I had been saving until I was alone—and carefully split the top, pulling out folded pages scribbled with thick black ink.

Nashville, the first city I loved, was in the midst of a mayoral campaign, and our friends at the Power Project were busy speaking out at public meetings and planning an Urban Plunge for the candidates. Andrew had joined them at several meetings and wrote, "Last week, Richard and I watched as Alonzo asked questions of the mayoral candidates. They were mostly really political and annoying, and Alonzo had to keep telling them: 'Gentlemen, I will not ask you again. Please answer the questions.'"

Andrew was getting more involved with the outreach ministry at our church, Otter Creek. The ministry leaders had a knack for mobilizing churchgoers to serve overlooked and discarded people. Charlie had given one of them a copy of the words Andrew and I had shared at the rally—"Take a look at what these students are doing!" he said—and the outreach leader had found us the next week at church.

Andrew joined a small group with one of the outreach ministers after I left for London. The group was reading a new book by an intentional community in North Carolina called the Rutba House about "the twelve marks of a new monasticism." The book described living toward a world in which the poor are actually blessed. It spoke of reviving monastic rhythms of contemplation and action, solitude and community. Practitioners moved their attention to "the abandoned places of Empire,"[7] lived simply, and focused on the work of reconciliation, hospitality, nonviolence, creation care, and community.

In his letters to me, Andrew talked about attending a New Monastic conference in Indianapolis and discovering Thomas Merton, a Trappist monk, peace activist, and author. I wrote back about reading Day and visiting an intentional community in Northumbria, where I was moved by their vows of vulnerability and availability to God and others. Something in us was stirring, pulling us like a powerful magnet to models of life that stepped out of consumerism's distractions and into more intentional and contemplative rhythms.

That summer, our letters carried a certain charge. "This is what you and I share in," wrote Andrew. "Right now, as you read this, you are somewhere in Europe—probably London. Right now, I am somewhere in the United States of America. And though it seems absurd to most, there is a God breathing through us, taking us to frightening places, beautiful places where we learn, through victory and failure, frustration and joy, that our work is for the sake of something so much greater than we can know."

I wrote him back on coffee-stained napkins and pressed leaves and flowers between them. This was, of course, the age of internet cafés and flip phones. The phone I was issued by my study-abroad program had no texting capabilities and could make only local calls. So we wrote to each other, and our words blazed with possibilities. I had dreams of love and love lost, and I sometimes woke in a sweaty dread that I would hurt the people I cared for. Longing lodged in my bones, heavy as lead, light as hope.

I was falling for Andrew.

Streetlamps lit my way back to the residence hall in the moonless night. I climbed to my top bunk, pulled the thin starched sheets over me, and listened to the intermittent whirrs of buses and taxis outside the window. A flood of gratitude for the acts of kindness I received—letters from home, free gifts of baklava, tender hands massaging the knots on my foot—welled up in my chest, spilling out into silent tears of thanks that dampened my pillowcase.

Dissent

Like Nashville, the London I had come to love had a history that was often glazed over in travel guides. There were peasant revolts, vagrancy laws, and a prosperity that was financed, in part, through the colonization and exploitation of countries like India, South Africa, Australia, and the Americas.[8] Eager to pay homage to the international underside of Britain's history, I took a solitary pilgrimage to the statue of Gandhi in Tavistock Square in Bloomsbury. The oil-bronzed prophet sat cross-legged with his eyes fixed low. As the light inched out of the park and sank behind a curtain of buildings, I pondered the strangeness of the empire Gandhi brought to its knees, enshrining him among the pigeons.

The semester before I graduated, I was captivated by Gandhi's role in sparking the Indian independence movement that used nonviolent civil disobedience to challenge Britain's colonization and rule of India. One of the many unjust laws Britain had passed was a law that made it illegal for Indians to gather and sell their own salt—a naturally occurring mineral and staple in their diets. They were forced to buy it from British rulers who levied a significant salt tax. In 1930 Gandhi organized a Salt March during which tens of thousands of people joined him in marching to the Arabian Sea where he picked a lump of salt out of the coastal muds and challenged British law and its legitimacy. I was amazed by his boldness. "You may never know what results come of your actions," Gandhi is attributed with saying, "but if you do nothing, there will be no results." Millions followed suit, and more than sixty thousand Indians, including Gandhi, were arrested. The arrests, of course, weren't just about salt—the salt was symbolic of a greater economic independence that had been stripped away by colonial rule. The tide began to turn when a group of peaceful

Indian demonstrators were beaten by British-led Indian police forces. Police relentlessly clubbed nonviolent Indians who buckled and crumpled into the mud like pummeled dough. News of these events spread across the world, prompting global outcry against Britain, but it took an additional seventeen years for the Indian people to win their independence.

My next pilgrimage was to a more modern critique of Britain on the side of a building in North London where Banksy's "Cash Machine Girl" was freshly inked. The stencil depicted a young girl being lifted up and pulled into an ATM by a robotic arm. The work pointed to the more sinister side of the banking and financial systems that made this great city possible.

I saw a very different side of London when I attended Mass at a Roman Catholic church called Brompton Oratory with the other study-abroad students. A deceptively humble edifice served as the outside of the church, and I was not prepared for what waited behind its cedar doors. As we stepped in, the hallway gave way to a stunning sanctuary. The air inside was smoky with the smell of frankincense. Tiered domes towered two hundred feet high, and marble columns climbed the walls. Gold, rustic red, and turquoise whispered warmth into the space. We sat in the back pews as the priest began to recite the liturgy in Latin. At the altar, candles glowed. Mesmerizing voices from the choir echoed across the columns, rising and curling like the incense smoke that blurred the rays of light pouring down.

Unable to make out the ancient words, my mind drifted. Surely there was some seed of truth and reverence in this liturgy. Surely there was sacredness in the splendor of the sanctuary. But something in me longed for simplicity. As the incense wafted upward, I wondered what religion was for. Was its purpose to obtain some amount of inner peace or sense of transcendence in a crumbling world? Was it to pacify the masses with "pie in the sky when they die," as American labor organizer Joe Hill countered?[9] Was it for spiritual salvation or political, social, and economic liberation? And how is religion to interact with the underside of history—with the realities of injustice, colonialism, capitalism, and more?

I couldn't experience the sacrament of Communion at that church's Mass, no matter how awestruck I was by its beauty and sense of tradition. It was while visiting Gandhi's statue and Banksy's stenciled artwork, while sharing my food with another man on the streets, that I felt a sense of communion with those who had been broken and poured out, where I felt the spirit of resistance breathing and beckoning.

I had no idea what my life would look like when I arrived back in the States. But I was learning that whenever I had extra food and coats, I needed to open my hands a little wider to my neighbor. I was learning that every small act of kindness matters and that kindness lived out on a systemic level is justice. I was being drawn to a descending and dissenting God and would never be the same.

3

BROKEN SOIL

IT WAS THE STEAMY PART OF JULY after I had arrived back from London, and the Carolina air was stifling. I tried to move on the faded flower-print couch but couldn't. Something was weighing me down. Every limb was an immovable hunk of meat.

My ankle screamed with torment, as if something was ripping it apart from the inside out—tendons, cartilage, bone, all splintering open. Panic fissured through me, and my heart thrashed against my chest. I gulped in air but couldn't get enough.

The muggy living room lifted from its axis, tilted, and spun. Somewhere above me, two figures were trying to calm me, trying to help slow my breathing.

"Breathe in," one of them said. "Now hold it for one, two, three, and out . . ."

Nothing helped. My parents offered me a paper bag, but my hands tingled with pins and needles. They curled into mummy-like claws, contorted, I would later learn, by the dangerously low levels of carbon dioxide in my blood caused by hyperventilation following a second invasive ankle surgery.

37

I don't remember my dad kneeling on the rug beside me. I don't remember the sirens or my mom opening the door for the paramedics. I don't remember being lifted onto the stretcher and deposited into the ambulance. I don't remember what they did to bring me back or how long I was in the hospital. I only remember waking up to cold sweats on that same flower-print couch sometime later.

For days I was laid out in the living room, supervised around the clock, coming in and out of consciousness. Showers were impossible. I felt encased by the smell of my own unwashed body, sticky with summer sweat. Bouts of nausea washed over me. A sleeve of saltines and a can of lukewarm Sprite became regular fixtures on the mahogany coffee table. The nerves in my ankle were jumbled like the wires of an old, broken TV. Moments of clarity peaked when the pain sharpened, when my stomach and bowels snarled and turned in on themselves.

It was light, it was dark.

I was in, I was out.

All the times I had felt invincible seemed eons away. I was brittle. Breaking. Broken. My experiences with troubled family members and my friends on the streets taught me that people could shatter. But now, falling to pieces was my story too.

Some days later, I woke up in the middle of the night gripped by piercing cramps. I curled into a ball. The ceiling fan above me creaked with each rotation. Darkness encompassed me while slivers of moonlight crept through slanted blinds. Suddenly, something in me separated. I was outside my body, weeping. I saw the invincible, cleaned-up version of me standing far away on a distant shore while the real, shattered me was dragged beneath the surface. I heard myself scream, then howl. A sea of pain. A light clicked on and my dad rushed to my side.

"What's wrong?" he begged. "Look at me, hon, look at me. What's happening?"

I couldn't speak, couldn't open my eyes. I unleashed anguishing howls. He rushed to get my brother and they lifted me up, carried me to the car, and laid me across the back seat. They sped through the night to the hospital. Every bump jolted my body, but I was no longer myself. I was the shell of a broken human awash in blinding pain.

My dad and brother carried my wailing body into the hospital, and a nurse waved them back to a cold metal exam table stretched over with a thin paper sheet smelling of latex and steel. Gloved hands gripped my arms and legs and tried to straighten me as my howl heightened into a scream.

"No!" I shouted and began to sob.

When I blacked out, they managed to take an X-ray of my stomach and intestines, but when I came to again, I heard my screaming resume. Two nurses began tearing off my clothes, trying to turn me over on the table.

"Stop! Stop it!" I yelled, hysterical and confused. It took at least two nurses to hold me down while a third pierced my skin with a needle and shoved an enema into me. Before the sedative hit, humiliation coursed through me. After they finished, my scream melted into sobs.

I was discarded on the exam table—bent, whimpering, half-clothed. The thin sky-blue curtain was half open. I shivered, sobbing alone, and it all went dark again.

Held

A week and a half later, finally out of the hospital, I couldn't shake the feeling of separation, the smell of latex, steel, and sweat.

Thanks to medical intervention and my parents' selfless care, I was coming back to myself. I had made it to the other side of two dangerous post-op conditions: insufficiently medicated pain that caused my body to go into shock, and ileus—an obstruction of my intestines due to the anesthetics and meds. I was still, however, trying to bury my feelings of helplessness and a strange sensation of shame.

How had I come unhinged so easily? If I hadn't had health in-surance, a family to care for me, and a home where I could recover, what might have happened?

"I can't believe you almost died twice," Andrew said over the phone. I still wasn't sure if this was a small exaggeration or not, but there was enough truth in it to make us both shudder.

Andrew was driving from Nashville to visit. We hadn't seen each other since the night before I boarded the plan for London. It's strange how distance can deepen the chemistry between two people. Something between us had shifted, though we hadn't yet named it.

Andrew grew up in southern New Jersey across from a peach orchard. He moved to Nashville to attend Lipscomb, and we first met through a mutual friend after a church service my junior year. We later took a creative writing class together and both gravitated toward each other's writing. Then came the year of friendship: more shared classes, kayaking misadventures, retreats to a mon-astery, study sessions at coffee shops and parks.

As our friendship flourished, I noticed there was a depth to him that intrigued me. He wrote poetry and songs and introduced me to musicians Leonard Cohen and Tom Waits. We both shared a commitment to social justice and an interest in contemplative spirituality. His family attended a small, conservative Church of Christ congregation similar to my own. We were brought up with many of the same values, but we both found those values expanding. In high school, as the war in Iraq was beginning in early 2003, Andrew found himself in a crisis of faith. His atheist and agnostic friends opposed the war, and so did he. A few of them traveled to Washington, DC, to demonstrate with half a million others against the invasion. Meanwhile, at his church, some of the ministers were using the pulpit to beat the drums for war. He carried his crisis and convictions with him to Nash-ville, and then came our friendship, the rally, the chemistry, the letters.

The first night of Andrew's visit to South Carolina, we stayed up late watching movies on the couch. He smelled fresh and musky, like chopped cedar after rain. At some point our fingers found each other and interlaced for the first time. I leaned into him on the couch, my back against his chest. He put one arm around me and continued to hold my hand with the other.

Sitting there, being held, feeling the rising and falling of his chest, I felt safe. I didn't feel like the crumpled shell of a person I was on the hospital table. I felt loved. I felt like I was enough, even in my broken, withered state.

"Tell me a story," I said, still a bit loopy from the new meds, wanting to prolong our time on the couch. I loved his mind, his ideas, how there was a lilting quality in the words that rolled off his tongue. After some made-up tales, we both grew quiet. His eyes caught mine, and we leaned together and kissed.

Welcome Home

I moved back to Nashville a few weeks later, and instead of applying to physical therapy schools, I was a patient. In college, I had been drawn to physical therapy not only because it made sense to me and would give me the lifestyle I wanted but also because I felt called to the vocation of healing. I had been shifting courses, however, since I reread the prophets, heard the statistics in Dr. Camp's class, stumbled upon the offices of the Power Project, and was hollowed by my own sense of powerlessness and need. I felt I was being called to a different kind of healing, but I was searching for where that calling would lead me.

I started looking for a job that didn't require too much walking and cobbled together a few part-time gigs. In my spare time, Andrew and I started teaching a poetry and creative writing class at Room In The Inn, the homeless services nonprofit Charlie had founded decades earlier. I lived for that class, the people who attended, and the friendships we formed. I dreamed of finding a job that would let me work on the streets full time.

As the holidays neared, I found myself doing rotations at a bookstore's calendar kiosk in the heart of the Green Hills Mall. The mall, a high-end shopping mecca, is in one of Nashville's most affluent neighborhoods. The calendar kiosk was located across from The Body Shop and Victoria's Secret, and the manufactured scent of exotic, fruity, floral perfumes overwhelmed my senses. Heels clicked with importance across glassy tile floors. Cash registers chimed like church bells and echoed across the hollow, two-story sanctuary. Everyone who came to the kiosk seemed hurried. Shopping bags dangled from their wrists and arms like bangles.

Days spent between the wealth of my workplace and the poverty of our class downtown left me dizzy. What was even more disorienting is that I knew these women, cuffed to their most recent purchases, were just like me. Did I not still have moments where I envied them? Had I not also worshiped at the feet of shiny gods?

"We are meant to be with the poor," Dorothy Day wrote, "and the distractions of the mighty should be a warning to us: that we not be blinded by their glitter."[1]

"You coming to the rally?" Andrew asked over the phone after my mall shift, shaking me out of my daze.

"Absolutely," I said, "see you there."

The Power Project was holding a "Welcome Home" rally at city hall to continue to push for more affordable housing with newly elected Mayor Karl Dean. A passing city bus left a rush of exhaust in its wake as I walked toward the stately, familiar columns. I hugged Andrew and our friends from the Power Project and then saw Tasha, whose photos had pulled me in.

Tasha's eyes lit up. "I was hoping to see you," she said. "We're starting a street paper and getting things off the ground with a meeting next week. Wanna come?"

Tasha and a handful of others were about to launch *The Contributor*. The paper would feature stories about homelessness and poverty and the writing and artwork of people who had experienced life on the streets. It would also offer employment for vendors who would buy each paper for twenty-five cents, sell them to customers for a dollar, and keep the profits. Within a year, Andrew would become the editor, and within a few years, *The Contributor* would become the largest street paper in North America.

After the rally, I spotted someone I had read about months earlier. After reading Dorothy Day, I searched for local Catholic Worker communities and found a website for the Nashville Greenlands. The founder of the community, Karl Meyer, was a leading figure in the Catholic Worker movement and had known Day personally. His name appeared in her letters and in the indexes of her writings. Despite his far-reaching reputation, he was a small-framed man with large silver glasses, a neatly trimmed silver beard, and simple jean overalls. He was a war-tax resister, pacifist, anarchist, carpenter, urban farmer, and a deeply religious agnostic. Karl had been arrested over fifty times and spent several stints in prison for his civil disobedience.

I walked up to him and introduced myself. "I've read a lot about you," I said. I extended my hand and he shook it heartily.

"And I've seen you," he responded, referring to my work with the Power Project. Karl introduced me to Pam Beziat, his counterpart in running the Greenlands community, which included several houses in North Nashville. Pam was a Quaker and an avid farmer, and while her day job was nursing, her record of civil disobedience and jail was impressive in its own right.

A month later, Andrew and I joined Karl and Pam for lunch in Karl's humble home in the distressed neighborhood of North Nashville. He had resourcefully restored his house by hand, along with several others on the block. Nearly everything we ate came from their gardens: winter greens, beets, chestnuts, and canned pears sprinkled with cinnamon. A steaming kettle sat in the center of the table. Karl showed us recent copies of the *Catholic Worker* newspaper, hundreds of books carefully tucked into dusty bookcases with glass doors, and his yard that had been converted into an urban garden nearly two decades before.

"When I first started the Greenlands," he said as we toured the wild yet meticulously organized yard, "I came to give life to vacant houses. I didn't buy houses with people in them," he explained, referring to the developers who would come years later to gentrify and flip the neighborhood for profit. He found the houses that were sitting empty, at risk of being demolished, and made them livable. "And can you believe it," Karl said, his voice rising in pitch and excitement. "This lawn was just sitting here, doing nothing but growing weeds. But look at it now! We've got fruit trees, chestnuts, blackberries, black raspberries, gooseberries, and every vegetable you can imagine!" In addition to being a haven for plants and wildlife, the Greenlands was also home to a network of organizers, activists, and others committed to a life of peace, justice, simplicity, and environmental sustainability. I was in awe. I didn't know then what role the Greenlands would come to play in my life and had no idea that Andrew and I would join the community several years later.

Boom and Crash

I was enamored with the simplicity and sustainability of the Greenlands. But at my mall job, surrounded by opulence, cynicism began to creep in. I was beginning to understand the poverty of wealth.

I was also beginning to experience meaning in our writing class downtown. During every session, I found myself staring straight into the talented, wind-burnt faces of the people who were teaching me about life, love, resilience, and resistance.

"Have you ever been homeless?" asked Ray Ponce De Leon, a brilliant satirist, and one of our regulars.

"I haven't," I replied.

"Good," he said. His carob eyes sat beneath an oversized stocking cap rolled sloppily above his feathery gray brows. "I hope you never have to be."

Another man, Matthew, rarely made eye contact with us or spoke up. His skin was the color of smoked caramel, and he hid himself behind black-framed glasses. He was well accustomed to being invisible, to being told he was nothing. But he could write. He wrote about loneliness, about hunger, about watching his grandmother try to make ends meet by working long hours at a grocery store seven days a week.

"To express," said Matthew in a moment of insight and courage, "you must have a soul, right?"

That night, I lit candles in my room and settled into a round cushioned chair. It was the first winter I had friends who were sleeping outside in the cold, and I didn't know what to do. On frigid nights, I spoke their names aloud as a kind of litany: Ray. Randall. Sheila. Matthew. I read a Thomas Merton quote over and over like a prayer: "My intention is to give myself entirely and without compromise to whatever work God wants to perform in me and through me."[2]

I flipped to a blank page in my journal, feeling helpless. The seeds that had sprouted in me were lacing roots into the broken soil of my life. The brokenness I came to know after my ankle injury in college, in London, and on the faded flower-print couch opened me up even more to the brokenness of the world around me. "I will fast from wealth, deny it in my life, and pursue justice, peace, and the indwelling of the kingdom of God on earth," my blue ink vowed in youthful sincerity.

The small house I rented with friends from college had fickle pipes and little heat, but it offered the warmth of community. All winter long, I wore my mother's knitted hats and retro navy snow boots from the 1970s. My bills piled up, and I learned to get by on twenty-five dollars in groceries every week with ramen noodles as a staple. I started writing for *The Contributor* and joined the small group at Otter Creek Church with Andrew and a crew of young parents who were deeply concerned about social and environmental issues.

We all knew the current system was broken, and we were hungry for a new way of life. As we learned about new monasticism and tried to put pieces of it into practice, gas prices began to rise, further pinching my budget. They climbed from $2.65 a gallon to $3.12, $3.80, $4.00. The global financial system was in the process of collapsing and an economic recession was underway.

It comes as no surprise that capitalism—a system that vacillates between cycles of boom and crash—continually produces situations of crisis. Like the housing bubble of the early 2000s, a bubble can stretch only so far before it pops. It wasn't long before the housing bubble burst, leading way to the Great Recession of 2007–2009. The fallout of capitalism's crashes can be minor or severe, depending on the nature of the boom. Instead of sending ripples across everyone evenly like a stone thrown into a pond, these crashes are like a landslide hurtling into a stream. Those downstream—the poor, the marginalized, the working class—experience a drought while those upstream are initially shaken but soon have a new lake in which to play.

As capitalism's newest crisis was wreaking havoc on the economy, our political system was being ravaged by what some called "crony capitalism"—an ethically nefarious alliance between powerful corporations and people in public offices. We saw this with Monsanto, a corporation that raked in billions by manufacturing pesticides and herbicides like Roundup, genetically modifying crops, and patenting seeds.[3] They ran small farmers out of business and paved the way for genetically modified organisms to hit the plates of nearly every household in America, but they were protected by lawmakers who received campaign contributions, kickbacks, and job opportunities in return. We also saw this with Corrections Corporations of America, the largest for-profit private prison corporation in the United States, now rebranded as CoreCivic. They received taxpayer dollars through government contracts to run private jails, prisons, and detention centers for

46

immigrants and asylum seekers. For every bed they fill, for every cost and service they cut, their profit increases.

One Sunday afternoon as I was talking with my mom on the phone, these national trends of privatization hit home. She told me that the small hospital my father worked for in South Carolina had been bought by one of the largest for-profit hospital chains in the country.

"Your dad's been going over the contract for a few days now," she said. "He can't sleep and has been sick to his stomach about the changes. The contract has little emphasis on patients and even less concern for the physicians."

"What's dad gonna do?" I asked. Growing up, my parents had always taught me to do the right thing and advocate for the underdog, regardless of the cost. When one of our more vulnerable family members wasn't getting the treatment or care they deserved, my mom went to bat for them, and anyone she went up against trembled. But my dad was nearing the end of his career as a pediatrician. What choice did he have?

"One of the most respected doctors he works with said he'd resign if he had to sign the contract as is," she said, "but your dad isn't sure what to do. He certainly can't practice on his own at this point. He just wants to care for his patients."

Perhaps our system wasn't so much broken as it was working exactly how it was supposed to work, benefiting those at the top for whom it was created.

Perhaps our system wasn't so much broken as it was working exactly how it was supposed to work, benefiting those at the top for whom it was created.

"If You Take It Seriously"

In all of this, Andrew and I were engaged and married. We said our vows and cut the cake on an unusually cool August evening. We moved in together, combined our book collections, and watched every dime. The week after we were married, I started the job of my dreams—a job that would pay me to work full time on the streets. I would serve as an AmeriCorps VISTA—a Volunteer in Service to America—for one year, maybe two, at Park Center's Homeless Outreach Program in Nashville.

As part of AmeriCorps, I would have a "living stipend" of just over $9,000 a year. At the orientation for AmeriCorps, we were all asked to pledge allegiance to the flag and take a vow to America, both of which I declined. I was beginning to understand that my ultimate allegiance was to something beyond a flag and a nation that defined itself by artificial borders.

Park Center, a mental health nonprofit, was home to our outreach team. We specialized in working with people on the streets who struggled with severe and persistent mental illness. In other words, we worked with the poorest of the poor, the sickest of the sick. Or at least that's how I thought of it then.

Jeannie Alexander, whom I was most excited about working with, started at Park Center around the same time I did. She was a tattooed mystic, a modern-day version of Dorothy Day or St. Francis with her dark hair cut short into a Joan of Arc–style bob. She came from serving as the director of the Power Project for a few months over the summer and had recently worked with them to temporarily occupy an abandoned house owned by the Department of Housing and Urban Development (HUD). While government housing like that unit was sitting vacant, families were facing foreclosure, kicked out of their homes with all their belongings set out on the curb. On a searing day in May, Jeannie marched with a couple dozen people in a sweaty procession from city hall across the Jefferson Street Bridge to the economically ravaged area along Dickerson Pike. From there, they caravanned to the empty HUD home and "peacefully reclaimed it" for an unhoused family.

Jeannie sat on the front stoop of the newly occupied porch and looked into the camera of someone filming the action.

"We're here because the poor, to no small extent, are being crucified in the streets of America," she said without flinching. "Despite the wheels of government turning slowly in Nashville, there are a lot of people in this town who understand what a crisis we're in. . . . What we can't afford to do is nothing."[4]

In her former life, Jeannie was a corporate attorney with a background in philosophy. She was politically active but worked for a firm whose clients were, in her words, "basically the devil." After a series of dreams and rereading the gospel, she realized she couldn't keep climbing up society's ladder. In reflecting on the gospel, she had this to say:

> After I read it I thought, wow, this is absolutely, if you take it seriously, take it on its face, not as platitudes or metaphor, it was the most radical thing I've ever read in my life—the most radical thing and it shook me to my core. . . . I walked up to my office and I gave my notice. . . . And I also, in reading not just the gospel but also the prophets as well, realized that God, working through history, shows a preferential option for the poor. Over and over again. Who does God choose? God chooses the prostitute, God chooses the murderer and the felon, God chooses the leper, God chooses the outcast. God chooses the poor. So I left my career, lost my house, lost all my money, lost everything, everything that I thought mattered. And by doing that, I gained everything that truly does matter.[5]

Outlaws

Our office at Park Center was on the second floor of an old, red-domed Presbyterian church. In our wing of the building, there was no air conditioning and no heat. Our desks were clustered beneath high ceilings and a series of ten-foot windows flanked by wood-paneled walls. We hauled a couple electric heaters up the stairs in the winter and set up fans in the summer.

Our team worked closely with the residents at Tent City, the largest encampment in Nashville and the source for many of

Tasha's photos. On my first visit to the camp, thick morning fog held around trees and tents, emanating from the banks of the Cumberland River. Jeannie and I walked the well-worn footpath along the railroad tracks and chain-link fence toward the river. Ironweed radiated purple from both sides of the path. To our right, a lattice of summer-worn trumpet vines climbed enormous concrete columns, reaching toward the interstate bridge high above our heads. As we neared Cowboy's impressive shanty, fully equipped with a porch and a wood-burning stove, his cats ran out to greet us, rubbing against our jeans.

"Don't mind them cats," Cowboy shouted from his covered porch. "They help with the rats!"

Before we got to the river, the trail hung a sharp left into a patch of woods and then opened to a clearing. At the entrance to a sprawling camp stood a wooden-pallet fence whose planks were engraved with an excerpt from Isaiah. "Enlarge the place of your tent," it read. "Stretch your tent curtains wide, do not hold back; lengthen your cords, strengthen your stakes" (Isa. 54:2).

As the sun began to burn off the fog, a man who introduced himself as Papa Smurf, and apparently took Isaiah literally, welcomed us and proudly showed us around his kingdom.

Smurf was a carpenter by trade and a self-proclaimed hillbilly by birth. I too had hillbilly in my lineage, a gift from my grandmother, who was the Appalachian daughter of a coal miner. But as I learned from my grandmother, hillbilly is more than blood. It's a disposition. It's a fierce hankerin' to be free. It's the uncanny ability to see humor and possibilities in the mundane. It's being able to "squeeze a quarter so tight the eagle screams," as the saying goes. Needless to say, Smurf and I hit it off.

With a lit cigarette dangling from his lips and a Natty Ice beer in hand, Smurf had a sturdy build and thick tattooed forearms. Two squinting, sky-colored eyes peered from beneath a bandana tied Willie Nelson style around his fluffy gray hair. While his personality was larger than life, his stature was modest at just over five feet.

The main part of Smurf's camp consisted of massive blue tarps tied together with ropes and bungee cords. They sheltered a forty-by-forty-foot area that held three individual tents, a common area, a food pantry, and a guest room used to provide hospitality. Gravel was spread evenly across the ground to keep mud at bay, and generator-powered lights were strung about the interior. In the center of the space, a fifty-gallon drum was transformed into a wood-burning stove whose exhaust pipe led out of a hole in the patchwork canopy. Around the pipe, tarps blistered away from the heat.

Outside the main part of the camp, there was a grill, a swing, a wood stack, and a chicken coop. There was also a clearing that served as Smurf's workshop and showroom for his handmade wooden crosses suspended from wire lines. "I call 'em 'Crosses for a Cause,'" he said with pride. "I start here with whatever pieces of wood the good Lord sends," Smurf explained. "I sand 'em down real good till the natural grains and colors come through. And then, ladies," he said with a dramatic pause, "I make 'em shine!"

He pulled out a large can of polyurethane that he used to coat each cross in layer upon layer until the proper shine was achieved. Just then, a woman emerged from the path, stepping into the workshop with us. Smurf gestured to her with a bow.

"And this," he said, locking eyes with his partner, "is the most beauteous woman in the world." Teresa blushed and eyed him back with a smile.

She was endearingly nicknamed "Mother Teresa" and was, at the time, searching high and low for their pet rooster, Natty, who was loved and loathed by other residents. The missing rooster was raised solely on hot dogs and beer and was so fierce that he once attacked a police officer who wandered past the fence.

As Smurf and Teresa walked us back beneath the tarps, he began to whisper and shushed us so we wouldn't wake the current occupant of their guest-room-turned-hospital-wing—an uninsured mummy of a man who was bound up in casts due to a broken neck and two shattered arms. He was slowly being nursed back to health by Mother Teresa, with the help of—you guessed it—hot dogs and Natty Ice.

That night, images flooded my mind as I stretched and iced my still-sore ankle. I pictured myself being carried when I couldn't walk. Andrew's fingers lacing in and out of mine. Karl and Pam at Greenlands, sowing seeds of resistance in abandoned lots. Jeannie, unflinching, sitting on the stoop of a reclaimed house. Driftwood crosses hanging in an outlawed camp. The cast-bound man.

I had learned that we're all closer to breaking than we think. But I was also learning that we're a hell of a lot stronger too.

4

DOWNHILL

BEHIND THE BRICK- AND ROCK-FACED EXTERIOR of my childhood church stood a playground made of wood and primary-colored plastics. The playground at that Church of Christ congregation was nestled in the rolling foothills of South Carolina. There was a cherry-red slide, a swing set, and monkey bars that all kept watch over a hill that sloped sharply down some forty feet to a creek. On one side of the water was a strip of shrubs and trees, and on the other side was an embankment that climbed up to a fenced-off highway.

After each Sunday service, my church friends and I would race out back to play while the grown-ups mingled inside. One day, my friend and I laid flat at the top of the hill, folded our arms across our chests, and rolled down, tumbling recklessly over dandelions and clover. Halfway down the hill, we rolled sideways and came to a stop, our hearts pounding, heads dizzy, giggling at the pieces of dried grass in our hair. Our parents told us to stay away from the creek. The hill was our border. Uphill was good and safe. Downhill was bad—off-limits.

But who on earth hasn't broken a rule?

That Sunday, my friend and I crept down to the bottom of the hill in grass-stained dresses, dizzy with defiance. We peered through the trees and tip-toed near the creek's edge on a flat rock shelf. A canopy of green crowded out the light, and as our eyes adjusted, our focus fell on a clothesline fixed between two trees. On the line were freshly hung mismatched socks, a yellowed t-shirt, small Pepto-Bismol pink shorts, and a blue checkered button-up.

A rush of adrenaline flooded my senses. *We are not supposed to be here*, I thought. "Come on!" I said, pulling my friend's arm. "Come on!" And up we ran.

I still don't know who called that narrow patch of woods home. All I know is that I was told that the creek and whatever was down the hill were unsafe. I was told to stay away. I never saw their faces, never looked anyone in the eye. Did anyone from our church?

Sometime after seeing the clothesline, I remember coming to church one Sunday to see that the brush and trees downhill had been completely cleared. I couldn't believe it. The earth next to the creek was bare, the clothesline a distant memory. Did someone at church clear the area to run people off? What happened to the people and their belongings? Later, as an adult, I would hear that some church members justified the brush removal as a marketing ploy—a way for the church to have greater visibility from the highway. But the take-away for me as a child was the feeling of separation. On the one hand, I was taught that God loved and welcomed everyone. On the other hand, I was taught to fear and avoid people who didn't look and smell like me.

The Notice

Back in Nashville, September was balmy, like the slowly cooling air of an oven. While Smurf's camp was well organized, much of Tent City was in major need of help. Among the thistles and trumpet vines were mountains of trash, mildewed heaps of clothes, and mounds of empty beer bottles strewn across large swaths of land. The development of a condo on a bluff towering above the camp sent a scourge of rats down to harass the residents. But the rats weren't the primary threat.

The footsteps of uniformed police officers pounded the path to Tent City, kicking up clouds of dust that were slow to settle. One officer held a laminated eviction notice proclaiming that the residents were to vacate the property by September 22, 2008. He hammered the notice to a telephone pole near the entrance. Anyone who stayed at the camp past the deadline would be subject to prosecution.

Tent City had been a well-kept secret among Nashville's homeless community since at least the early 1980s. But in the early 2000s, people without housing were being driven off the streets by a "Please Help, Don't Give" campaign launched by downtown businesses and aimed at decreasing panhandling. The enforcement arm of this campaign was more police citations and arrests for petty offenses like trespassing and "obstructing the passageway"—a charge that could be applied to people sitting on sidewalks, sleeping beneath awnings, resting on the steps or stoops of downtown establishments, and more.

A nonprofit agency had a bus lot that backed up to the camp, and as Tent City's population grew, the staff became more concerned about sanitation and safety. They reached out to Public Works for port-o-potties and trash cans, but this request spurred conversations that led city officials to decide that the camp needed to close. After a string of media stories about the impending closure, however, the officials, hoping to avoid more bad press, reached out to service providers like Park Center, requesting that we provide social service referrals and resources for transitional and permanent housing to the residents.

Then, shortly after I started at Park Center, a drunken Labor Day brawl erupted at the camp. As the story goes, a newcomer had a little too much to drink during the festivities and made an unwanted pass at one of the women. An established resident stepped in, armed with a knife, and stabbed the newcomer, who was sent to the hospital and subsequently patched up. Tensions between the police and residents were already high, but that particular incident tipped the scales. It brought the officers to the camp, nailing the eviction notice to a pole.

Many of us in the outreach community were accustomed to police raids where tents were slashed, burned, bulldozed, or dragged off and thrown into a dumpster with little, if any, notice. If the residents were caught, they were cited or arrested. But at Tent City there were too many people and too many eyes were watching. Still, a date was set and city officials and the police weren't budging.

That Sunday, Andrew and I told the members of our church group about the notice.

"Where are they going to go?" I asked, thinking of Smurf, Teresa, Cowboy, and others. I knew we had to act. "The church cannot be content to play the part of a nurse looking after the casualties of the system," I said, quoting Catholic missionary and priest Donal Dorr. "It must play an active part both in challenging the present unjust structures and in pioneering alternatives."[1]

One of the outreach ministers in our group agreed. The next day, he reached out to the nonprofit located beside Tent City. After he talked with them, he called me. "Of course it's a mess down there," he said with empathy. "What would happen if we got some volunteers together to help them clean the place up?"

This outreach minister was the kind of guy who made things happen. And as a staff member at a wealthy church located just outside Nashville's city limits in the most affluent county in Tennessee, he had every resource at his disposal to do so. Within a week, a port-o-potty and dumpster had been installed. Then, we led a massive campwide clean-up with the residents and some local college students.

At the next meeting of the Metro Homelessness Commission, commission members requested that Mayor Karl Dean give outreach workers more time to find housing and resources. Dean obliged, setting the new closure date for November 1. After the announcement, September came and went. But it was clear that there was no way to find housing for all the residents before the looming deadline.

"Where are we going to go?" became the constant refrain at the camp.

Some of us discussed options for creative resistance. Jeannie reminded us of the tradition of naked protests enacted by women in Africa to shame powerful men. "If anyone wants to sue you and take your shirt," said Jesus in the Sermon on the Mount, "hand over your coat as well" (Matt. 5:40). As you can imagine, the idea of everyone going commando raised some eyebrows and was quickly struck down, despite the enthusiasm of a few.

I helped organize a rally at city hall with Jeannie, other outreach workers, and Tent City residents like Mama Bear, whose Cherokee roots gave her more claim to the land than anyone. News of the rally spread among homeless advocates, organizers, and students. News also spread among city officials who began to fear a public relations catastrophe.

Just hours before the rally was to take place on a chilly Friday in late October, Jeannie got a call from Charlie, who served on the commission. "Have you seen the mayor's press release?" he asked.

"No," Jeannie said. "Is it bad?"

"You're not gonna believe this," Charlie replied, "but he's giving the camp a reprieve!"

"Seriously?" she said, stunned by the news.

"Seriously," said Charlie.

We were astounded. Dean, under mounting pressure, had accompanied Charlie on a private tour of the camp to see the conditions and to meet the people that he and other city officials were about to evict. In a stunning turn of events, Dean decided to grant the camp a reprieve and hand the situation over to the Metro Homelessness Commission, who would form an ad hoc committee to decide the camp's fate.

In our elation, we folded one of our protest signs in half and converted it into an oversized thank-you card for Dean. Everyone signed the card in colorful marker scribbles. We gathered on the familiar city hall lawn with dozens of students, residents, concerned citizens, and reporters and announced that instead of having a protest, we would have a celebration.

A tearfully triumphant Mama Bear and her partner Pontiac addressed the crowd. "All we ever asked for was a chance," Pontiac said, "a chance to prove this city wrong about who we are. And today, that chance has been granted."

Move-Ins

The early November air smelled like chopped wood, mildew, and dog hair as I loaded the belongings of two more Tent City residents into my crimson 4Runner. Mike, Rebecca, and their loveable, smelly, old-as-dirt dog, Sheba, were finally moving into their own apartment. They were moving into an apartment complex with Mama Bear, Pontiac, and Harold, a man from the camp who had lived on the streets for longer than I had been alive.

"We're not gonna know how to act," said Mike from behind his inch-thick glasses during the ride. He was shaking with nerves. "How do we act?" Rebecca, a painter, sat in the back, cradling Sheba, who whimpered and whined. After we unloaded the trash bags packed with Mike and Rebecca's lives, I went to check on Harold.

"Hey man, how are things going?" I asked. He told me he was lonely as hell before his friends moved into the apartments next to him. "I brought you something," I said, holding his gifts behind my back. As he opened the door for me to come in, I noticed how bare his single-room efficiency still was. I made a mental note to call a church contact who was helping us furnish some of the apartments. Harold had a camping chair, a flipped over crate that served as a table, a small dresser and twin bed that came with the apartment, and a trash bag of dirty clothes in the corner. I handed him a vase full of reeds and a sizable framed picture of a prairie dancing in the wind.

His dust-brown eyes lit up, and creases like the feet of crows spread from his eyes. "These'll make it bearable in here," he said with the first smile I had seen from him in over a week. "They'll make it feel like home."

Years later, one of our interns would liken the experience of people moving into housing after years on the streets to the experience of veterans coming home from war. Sometimes coming home feels like gratitude, safety, healing. Other times, it can be disorienting. People like Harold leave a space of sheer survival, violence, struggle, and loss. They leave a community, broken as it may have been, and are dropped into a box that too often isolates them from the world. Sometimes that box is in a crowded apartment complex with paper-thin walls. Sometimes it's in a drug-infested neighborhood where people bang on doors at all hours of the night. When they are no longer busy surviving, they have to figure out how to spend their time so their trauma and demons won't catch up with them and devour them alive. First, the feeling of loneliness sets in. Next comes the aimlessness, the pressure, the bills. And then there's the survivor's guilt, that gnawing knowledge that many of their comrades are still out there, still surviving—or not.

The reality for some of our friends who make it off the streets is that housing alone isn't the magic bullet. Without community and support, and sometimes even with it, they merely leave one kind of poverty for another.

> *The reality for some of our friends who make it off the streets is that housing alone isn't the magic bullet. Without community and support, and sometimes even with it, they merely leave one kind of poverty for another.*

The next people to move in after Mike and Rebecca were Barbara and her boyfriend, Cheeseburger. Barbara was like a mother at the camp. Her warmth and care radiated through to everyone she met. She was in her early forties, had sun-aged skin, yellow-blonde hair, and crystal-blue eyes that held the light. On Christmas Eve, the whole newly housed crew was drinking heavily at Barbara's place. Perhaps they were celebrating. Perhaps they were medicating the feelings of loss that always came up around the holidays. But at some point during the festivities, Barbara became sick and couldn't stop throwing up.

We got the call the day after Christmas. I was out of town with Andrew's family and took the call while pacing around his sister's driveway in the cold.

The streets had not killed Barbara as we feared they would. She had choked to death on her own vomit in her new apartment.

Barbara's death sent waves of shock and grief through us all. The next week, our outreach team drove a despondent Cheeseburger and his friends to the funeral, held just outside the city in a tiny chapel with rigid wooden pews. A preacher who had never met Barbara or any of her friends presided over the service. For the next hour, he preached at us about the sins of the flesh, the dangers of the world, and how Jesus was the only ticket out of an eternity spent in hellfire and damnation. He assumed Barbara and all of us were wayward heathens needing to be washed in the saving blood of the Lamb. Anger rose in me as he spoke. He hadn't seen the way Barbara had cared for others. He hadn't seen the way others loved her, even in their damaged ways. Fury climbed from my belly into my throat and escaped from my eyes in briny tears of rage.

Halfway through the service, Cheeseburger got up and walked out. Jeannie and I went to stand with him in the cold as his trembling hands lit a cigarette.

"Barbara deserves better than this," he said with swollen, bloodshot eyes, exhaling a pillar of smoke. "We all do."

The Multitudes

As the weeks unfurled into months, a new litany of friends lived in my heart like prayer. Kandy. Lily. Cathy. Kentucky.

I met Kandy at Room In The Inn's foot clinic. The clinic was the brainchild of Jeannie and Robb, a gentle and devoted nurse practitioner with endearingly corny jokes. As I cared for her feet, Kandy told me she was raped as a child and was still trying to make sense of it. "I suppressed it till I was forty," she told me, gripping her cross necklace, "and then I broke."

I heard stories like hers every week as we washed feet, scrubbed dead skin with pumice stones, clipped gunky, yellow-brown nails, and massaged calloused, mangled soles. After a few months, I got over the smell and shock. Seeing people's feet revealed the severity of their condition—a condition that festered in the cracks of a system upon which others built wealth. After weeks, months, or years without care, a person's feet wither, rot, harden, and decay while the body is busy surviving. Dry socks, foot spray, and a "come back next week" sometimes felt like all we could offer people like Kandy. But perhaps there was more. I knew from the first feet I washed that there was something sacred about scrubbing off the grime, sloughing dead skin, and getting new calluses on my hands from trimming their thickened nails week after week. There was something holy about working their arches until my own hands ached. Had not others done this for me?

The next week, I met a bright-eyed two-year-old named Lily and her mother, Cathy, a single mother on disability, abandoned by the child's father. Cathy had no safety nets or family support. When most people think of homelessness, they level accusations that people are on the streets because they choose to be, because they made bad decisions. "If the homeless are hobos, junkies and bums," wrote Jeannie in *The Contributor*, "then I guess you could say Lily is the littlest bum."[2]

When the general public pictures someone on the streets, they imagine a shabby older man, perhaps a veteran with PTSD, pushing a cart. Lily was as far away from this stereotype as one could get—sober, beaming, innocent. Yet the fastest growing demographic experiencing homelessness, both in Tennessee and across the nation, was not self-medicating vets. It was families with children.[3]

And then there was Kentucky, the stereotypical homeless guy—the hippie-loving, train-hopping, bandana-wearing, PTSD-riddled Vietnam vet who pushed a shopping cart around East Nashville and slept on church stoops. Kentucky's buggy held a single crutch and several plastic bags with piss-yellow antiseptic mouthwash that he drank to drown his trauma, his shame. Mouthwash was, after all, cheaper than liquor, and you could buy it without an ID.

"I keep fillin' myself with this stuff," he told me one day. "I know I'm hurtin' myself, but I don't know what else to do."

Kentucky loved to tell me stories about all the church buildings he had wandered into over the years. Something always drew him to churches. It was as if he gravitated to the possibility of healing and forgiveness but couldn't allow himself to receive such grace. He didn't deserve it, he told me. He had done too much.

"The closest I ever got to being baptized," he said one day with a gummy grin, "was when I stumbled into a church one night when it was real cold. I was lookin' for a place to sleep, and without knowin' it, climbed down into the baptistry. The next morning, I woke up on the other side, soaked from my waist to my boots." He told me another story about spending the night on the pew of an unlocked Catholic church. Just before morning Mass, a man woke him up to invite him to stay for the service. "Nah," said Kentucky as he gathered his coat and stood up to leave. On his way out, he took a few long gulps of water from a bowl because his throat was parched. The man ran over to him and stopped him.

"Don't you know what that is?" he asked.

"Nope," Kentucky replied.

"That's holy water!" he exclaimed. Kentucky shrugged. Gradually, the man's offense melted into a smile. "Well, at least you're filled with the Holy Spirit," he said, patting Kentucky on the back. I marveled at this. Despite Kentucky's unwillingness to accept grace, it was as if grace was pursuing him.

A few months into our friendship, Kentucky was ready to give detox and rehab a try. One morning, I drove him to the VA hospital as his "DTs" and shakes were beginning to set in. He was worried about detox. "I nearly backed out a hundred times," he said. At a stoplight, I slid Pink Floyd's *Dark Side of the Moon* into my car's CD player. The first song began with the *tha-thump* sound of a beating heart joined by the sound of cash registers and helicopters.

"Girl, you know me," he said, grinning. We rolled down the windows and turned up the music. On my ride back, all I could think about was the worn and faded Pink Floyd shirt my Uncle Phillip wore before he climbed the attic stairs, ended his life, and sent shock waves through our family that rattle us still.

"The human soul doesn't want to be advised or fixed or saved. It simply wants to be witnessed—to be seen, heard and companioned exactly as it is."
—Parker Palmer

Kentucky didn't get sober after that visit, but he did, for a while, nearly a year later. "Here's the deal," says author Parker Palmer. "The human soul doesn't want to be advised or fixed or saved. It simply wants to be witnessed—to be seen, heard and companioned exactly as it is."[4]

Co-liberation

At Park Center, we were trained in a deeply relational approach to homeless outreach. The founder of our program was a student of Ken Kraybill, the Seattle native who helped develop this framework in the 1990s. Relational outreach understands that healing doesn't happen through transactions alone—through blankets, bus passes, and birth certificates. Healing happens through cultivating relationships of mutuality and trust.

In order to form these relationships, we were taught to meet people where they were geographically, mentally, emotionally, and spiritually. If someone was living in the rafters of an interstate underpass, we climbed the steep concrete incline and met them there. We were taught to accept people as they were, learn their names and stories, recognize their strengths, listen to their priorities, and work together as a team.[5] The people we met on the streets were not problems to be solved or cases to be managed; they were siblings, neighbors, and friends to be loved and journeyed with. I came to see our work as a ministry of accompaniment, of sharing the journey side by side. It was a ministry of proximity, of budding solidarity, of what we called co-liberation.

"If you have come to help me," aboriginal activist and educator Lilla Watson is attributed with saying, "you are wasting your time. But if you have come because your liberation is bound up with mine, then let us work together." Watson learned this lesson from her community, her elders, her people, and I was beginning to learn this lesson from my friends on the streets.

For years, beginning in my childhood church and continuing with the lessons I learned in society, I was taught to stay "uphill." But now, I was drawn downhill not because I had something to offer, not because I had the answers, solutions, or remedies to anyone's pain. I was drawn there because I had something to receive, something to learn. I was drawn there because that is where I found God moving most tangibly.

Through my friendships with people like Smurf, Kandy, and Kentucky, I was learning to let go, to trust God, and to open my hands a little wider to my neighbors. I was being saved—from myself and from a wayward society that told me my worth was bound up in what I accomplished, accumulated, and possessed.

I didn't know then that the coming years on the streets would both hollow and heal me, but I knew where I had to be. Down the hill. Down the footpath. Beneath the underpass. My healing would come from my wounds. It would come from community. It would come from below.

5

BURNING HEARTS

ON A WARM AND BRIGHT FEBRUARY AFTERNOON,
Jeannie practically bounced into our East Nashville office.

"Who wants to walk downtown today?" she asked. She smelled like patchouli and was wearing her favorite Chaco sandals with speckled socks. In a couple weeks' time, she would give those sandals away to a barefoot woman downtown and then walk barefoot herself until she replaced them.

Some of my coworkers shrugged at the invitation. They had work to do and cars to drive. But I caught the vibe along with one of our other colleagues.

As our trio walked downtown, we lost ourselves in conversation and handed out fresh socks and water to the people we passed. Our discussion gravitated toward our frustration with the well-established bureaucracy of city government, which we feared would "committee" itself to death before ever acting on lasting solutions for our friends at Tent City. We also discussed the "religious and nonprofit industrial complexes"—the faith communities and nonprofits that benefited from doling out services while maintaining the status quo. Instead of challenging the existing systems that perpetuated inequity, they knowingly or unknowingly propped them up. Despite the inspiring examples of ministers like Charlie and others, we had seen city officials, nonprofits, and so many faith communities fail our friends on the streets. We were disenchanted by organized religion and felt that so many churches applauded charity but failed to work toward justice. In these churches, it seemed that faith was relegated to the private sphere of personal morality, and the focus was on advancing their own institutions instead of embodying the gospel and its good news to the poor.

"I've been thinking," Jeannie said. "Park Center is its own secular nonprofit. They're funded by the government, and their funds have hoops that some of our people can't jump through. What if we started our own church on the streets with its own fund?"

We ruminated on Jeannie's proposal and followed up with a coffee date where Andrew joined us to dream and conspire. Like Jeannie, Andrew and I were drawn to the Christian anarchism of Dorothy Day and others. While anarchism is a loaded term with numerous meanings, it simply indicates what its etymology implies: *an*—without, *arch*—rulers or domination. While most anarchists are famous for their "no gods, no masters" stance, Christian anarchists hold more of a "one God, no masters" stance. They understand that their ultimate allegiance is not to a nation, a flag, or a president, but to a crucified God. They are first and foremost citizens not of their country but of the borderless kingdom of God.

Even the language of "kingdom" however, signified the lording of power over others. Perhaps what we needed was to embody the "kin-dom" or "commonwealth" of God, as *mujerista* and feminist theologians have asserted. Martin Luther King Jr. preferred the phrase "Beloved Community," and I would later resonate with the phrase "collective liberation" that I learned from the movement community.

Christian anarchism is an orientation to power. Rather than taking power and holding it *over* others, power is shared collectively.

Andrew and I were both raised in the Church of Christ—a self-proclaimed "non-denominational" denomination in which individual congregations were organized independently, with no centralized governing structure. Our churches had a level of freedom to make their own decisions—or at least the all-male elders and deacons did. Many leaders in our churches didn't trust politicians and were decentralized and anarchistic, for better or worse. David Lipscomb, founder of the Church of Christ–affiliated Lipscomb University, was arguably a Christian anarchist, something I'd become aware of through a riveting campus discussion during my sophomore year between three faculty members—a Christian anarchist, a Christian pacifist, and a Christian socialist. Andrew and I learned from all three.

Jeannie, Andrew, and I were also all drawn to liberation theology. Liberation theology emerged in both Latin America and North America in the 1960s and is rooted in the understanding that, in addition to personal implications, Scripture has social, economic, and political implications for Christians. Proponents of liberation theology argue that God is on the side of the poor and oppressed and that salvation isn't merely relegated to some otherworldly afterlife but also involves social, economic, and political liberation for the poor and oppressed in the here and now. These ideas called to us, and we wanted a place where we could explore what they meant for us today.

We circled back to Jeannie's idea of starting a church. It felt like the only thing that made sense. Jeannie and I could still work for Park Center, and Andrew and I could still attend services at Otter Creek Church, but we would have an outlet for this other part of who we were.

"What if we call the church Amos House?" Jeannie said. The prophet Amos was known for calling out exploitation, confronting the complacent, and exposing the emptiness of religion apart from sacrificial living. It was settled. We would start a church and call it Amos House. It could host a benevolence fund—the Mercy

Fund—that we would use for our friends who fell through the cracks of other systems, agencies, and faith communities.

Amos House would be a living, breathing experiment in what church could look like without steeples, walls, and paid clergy. It would be ecumenical yet rooted in the Catholic Worker tradition and rhythms of contemplation. It would be a haven for people who were in recovery from their own religious traditions. It would also be welcoming to everyone: students, teachers, gardeners, urbanites, activists, contemplatives, urban monastics, and Christian anarchists. Instead of cloistering ourselves off from the world, we would wander, living out our faith in tent cities, prisons, community gardens, and public squares. We would seek to live nonviolently, to speak truth to power, and to advocate for the rights of the outcast, exploited, and forgotten. We would wash feet together on the streets and serve Communion to anyone anywhere who wanted it, declaring that all are welcome at God's table.

We had no ambitions of rapid growth, the accumulation of property, or world domination. We would let the church start small as a mustard seed and grow organically. If Amos House ever stopped serving its purpose or people, if it ever got too big for its britches, we would close it. The point was not maintaining the institution; the point was a life of active, wrestling faith. Like the disciples walking on the road to Emmaus on Easter Sunday, we found Christ in the stranger, in the walking, in the breaking of bread. "Did not our heart burn within us?" (Luke 24:32 KJV), the disciples said after realizing the stranger was Christ.

> Like the disciples walking on the road to Emmaus on Easter Sunday, we found Christ in the stranger, in the walking, in the breaking of bread.

Maybe we were idealists. Maybe we had authority issues. Maybe both. But if we didn't pursue this, it would be as if there were a "fire shut up in [our] bones." We were "weary of holding it in," and indeed could not (Jer. 20:9).

Holy Week

Before Jeannie came to Nashville, she too had fallen in love with Dorothy Day and had become involved with the Open Door Community—a Catholic Worker house in Atlanta made up primarily of Protestants. I had read about Open Door and knew that during Holy Week the community took to the streets for twenty-four-hour blocks. They called this "Holy Week on the Streets"—a wandering vigil, a pilgrimage of sorts, to study Scripture in an undomesticated context.

Holy Week begins with Palm Sunday, the day when Jesus turns toward the city of Jerusalem, weeps over it, and enters into the public conflict that will lead to his execution. Instead of entering the city on a warhorse, Jesus rides a donkey. He mourns the way the city kills her prophets and fails to grasp the way of peace.

We decided that Holy Week on the Streets would be the inaugural event for Amos House. Every day, a different group of people would spend twenty-four hours on the streets praying, breaking bread, and journeying to symbolic places that were important to the lives of our friends on the streets. On Good Friday, we would invite a broader group to participate in an event called Citywide Stations of the Cross, journeying to the places where Jesus, in the guise of the poor, is accused, arrested, beaten, helped, condemned, and crucified in our city. We would journey to our own Gethsemanes, places where we fail to keep watch; to the offices of our own Pilates, who wash their hands of the fates of the poor; to our own Golgothas, where modern-day death sentences are doled out.

Before leaving, Andrew and I emptied our pockets and bags of everything but our state IDs, water bottles, Bibles, and journals. Each group would bring only one phone to use in case of an emergency. The point of all this was *not* to experience what it was like to be unhoused. The loneliness, isolation, and distress don't set in until later, until you know there's no foreseeable "out" for you, until you are worn down and your body and mind shift into

71

survival mode where every ounce of energy is employed to stay alive—or not.

As I was emptying my bag, I remembered a conversation I'd had with Davie, a big, burly sailor of a guy, at the Jefferson Street Bridge. One day, the group providing lunch ran out of forks and we were joking about having to eat with plastic knives.

"Makes me feel like John Wayne to eat a can of peaches with my pocketknife," he said, smiling. I laughed.

"I'll think of you whenever I eat my meals with a knife," I said.

Davie grinned at first, but then, his rough face turned stern. "You can think of me, of us, when you take a warm shower tonight too, because we don't get to do that." My face reddened.

On Wednesday of Holy Week, Andrew and I co-led a group with one of the men whose ashen feet I had washed at the foot clinic. We met in a parking lot littered with trash, and the group from the night before passed off a few blankets we could use. We introduced ourselves from our asphalt seats—three co-leads, three students, a Vanderbilt employee, and three grungy twenty-somethings from our friend Richard's community house. Then we set off.

Our first stop was city hall. We each took turns sharing about what our background with Christianity had been like and where we were in Scripture. We explored passages from Isaiah and discussed how Jesus was a kind of anti-king. "Jesus died the victim, abandoned to executioners with imperial power," wrote theologian Mark Lewis Taylor. "We can note an inescapable opposition between the life and death of Jesus, on the one hand, and imperial power on the other. To embrace and love the executed God is to be in resistance to empire."[1] We wrestled with how to live and respond to the "principalities and powers" of this world. What should our relationship with power look like? Was power always bad? Or was there something important about where power came from and how it was wielded?

It was nearing dinner time, and we split into two groups with the mission of finding food by searching for leftovers and panhandling. My group walked through an alley and found an un-locked gate guarding a few trash cans. We tore and picked through the bags before being chased off by a man in a lipstick-red apron. Next, we went to several restaurants where we were told meals were made to order with no leftovers. We sifted through more trash bags but found nothing edible. It was almost seven, just thirty minutes before our group's meet-up time, and we still had nothing. Our empty stomachs turned. A few of us nervously decided we would try panhandling.

I walked to the sidewalk in front of the library on the edge of a small park and began asking passersby for change. The first several people I asked said they didn't have anything or ignored me. One man who turned me down came back to offer a dollar bill.

"Get something to eat with this," he said with pity in his eyes.

Nearly half an hour later, I still had only one dollar when a man with rectangular glasses and a prominent goatee circled back around.

"Here you go," he said as he handed me a wad of cash, then smiled and walked away. I opened my hand and realized that he had given me a fistful of twenties.

"Thank you so much!" I yelled after him. But I felt a tinge of guilt. Would the man have shown the same generosity to someone who wasn't young, white, and female?

I took the cash to the others and we tallied up our finds. As expected, the community house guys had some success dumpster diving. They brought two bags of crusty dinner rolls, half a bag of popcorn, four large potatoes, and a box of off-brand snack cakes.

We decided we would use the money to buy pizzas for everyone in the park and some grape juice for Communion. We started invit-ing our friends on the streets to eat with us. By the time the pizza and juice arrived, there were over thirty people, and after dinner, we invited whoever wanted to stay to join us for Communion. About twenty people gathered in a circle as we read the passage from Luke about the Lord's Supper. We passed around the crusty dinner rolls and cups of grape juice and blessed them. As each person attempted to bite through the dinner rolls, laughter trickled around the circle. They were stale and rocklike but strangely perfect for our Communion. Did not our hearts burn within us?

After we finished, a man from the streets walked up to me. I had washed his feet a few weeks before and had tended the blood blisters and calluses that spotted his toes from his steel-toe boots. He took off his large navy jacket and insisted that I take it.

"It's gonna be cold tonight, and I can handle it," he said. "But you're gonna need this." I tried to talk him out of it as he pushed it toward me. "Nah, take it. I got a blanket where I sleep." I accepted his gift. What did it mean for him, a man so accustomed to receiving, to be able to offer this? I slid my arms into the still-warm jacket and rolled up the sleeves. I thanked him and told him I'd get it back to him at the next foot clinic.

When people downtown asked what our group was doing, one of the grungy guys would say, "We're looking for Jesus out here!" Or we'd explain that Jesus had entered the heart of the city during the week leading up to Good Friday and Easter, and we were trying to do the same.

We left the park around nine thirty and started the long walk to Tent City. In the inky night, streetlights blinked on and the city broadened and transformed. She took off her suit, shook out her hair, and breathed a little deeper.

When we got to Tent City, we hit the port-o-potties, thankful for free, accessible restrooms—despite the smell. As we trekked back to Smurf and Teresa's camp in the dark, we crunched over winter sticks on the path. Hugs and cookies welcomed us, and Smurf tossed more wood on the fire. Earlier in the week, when Andrew and I asked if our group could stay, they told us they wouldn't have it any other way. Their hospitality that night would solidify our lifelong friendship with them both.

"Here's these, honey," said Teresa, handing me a few blankets and pillows from their stash. We spread the blankets over the gravel floor in the main living area, and as we were bedding down, the current occupant of the hospital wing offered us his bed.

I slept for a while but woke up shivering around three thirty in the morning as the fire died down. By four we were all up. This was the hour that day laborers left their camps to line up at temp agencies hoping for work. We packed up our things and thanked our friends. "Come back anytime!" Smurf called out as we left.

After stopping by the port-o-potties once again, we headed to a day labor agency downtown. We were bundled up in our blankets like a band of ghostly monks floating down dreary streets. When we got there, we sat on the pavement between the "no trespassing" and "no loitering" signs, and I recounted stories I had heard from Smurf and others about the struggles of working day labor. We read through passages in the book of Jeremiah, talked about workers' rights, and spent the next hour—the coldest hour of the day—in silence. We journaled as cardinals chirped from holly trees and as the sky yawned awake, drenched in peaches and pinks. Gradually, the city sat up, stretched her arms, picked up her briefcase, and started another day.

We still had twelve dollars from the night before, and while we thought about going to a fast-food restaurant for breakfast, we decided we could stretch the funds further if we went to a gas station and bought a couple large cups of coffee to split, a loaf of bread, and supplies to make peanut butter and jelly sandwiches.

After breakfast, we went to a foot-washing service for Maundy Thursday and walked back across town where we had lunch under the Jefferson Street Bridge and read the story of the loaves and fishes being multiplied. Next, we went to the state capitol, where we wrestled with whether we were called to submit to the authorities as Paul wrote in Romans 13. How did this passage relate to the rule-breakers in Scripture like Jesus, who overturned tables and broke Sabbath laws? How did it relate to Peter and the other apostles who said, "We must obey God rather than human beings" (Acts 5:29)?

From the capitol, we walked to a downtown bank plaza and studied a passage together from the fiery book of James. "Now listen, you rich people, weep and wail because of the misery that is coming on you," we read. "Your wealth has rotted, and moths have eaten your clothes. Your gold and silver are corroded. Their corrosion will testify against you and eat your flesh like fire. You have hoarded wealth in the last days" (James 5:1–3). How did our society encourage us to accumulate wealth and possessions? What were we hoarding that others could use? What kind of people were these passages calling us to be?

Finally, we went to a downtown church to read the story of the rich man and Lazarus. But we didn't find Christ at the church. We found him in the stranger, the walking, the breaking of crusty, reclaimed dinner rolls. Did not our hearts burn within us?

Holy Week, Good Friday, and Easter came and went, leaving us all rocked, filled with a kind of hunger for the holiness and fire we had found on the streets. As we were still processing what we had experienced, we met Ben, the gnome of a man who nearly broke us all.

Better Resources

Ben was fifty-four with a rosy, cratered face, matted hair, a long gray-brown beard, fierce paranoia, a developmental disability, and a proclivity for talking with people who weren't actually there. He came from Cincinnati, where a police officer loaded him onto a Greyhound bus and sent him to Nashville because we had better resources. Ben landed at the Nashville Rescue Mission on a Thursday afternoon with eleven dollars in his pocket. A staff member who didn't know what to do with Ben called a police officer assigned to work with people on the streets. That officer then called Jeannie, begging her to do something with him.

"He's hamburger meat in there," said the staff member, who feared other guests at the shelter would take advantage of Ben.

When Jeannie got to the mission, a team from Mobile Crisis had just completed their assessment of Ben but said he wasn't sick enough for their services. The police officer insisted on referring him to the state mental health hospital, which would require medical clearance and blood tests. Jeannie spent the night with Ben at a local hospital, holding his sweaty, frightened hand, awaiting his results. At one point, he squeezed her hand and whispered, "I wish you would have been my mom."

That night ended with a referral to the mental health hospital by the treating physician, but the hospital turned him away.

"If he's not violent, if he's not an active danger to himself or others," they said, "there's nothing we can do for him."

Jeannie loaded Ben and his eleven dollars into her jeep and brought him to the office. While we tried to figure out what to do, Ben watched Japanese anime cartoons and played a game called Diamonds on my computer. "They keep me out of trouble," he said.

Later that day, Jeannie found Ben a spot in a transitional housing facility, but after staying one night he stormed out, gripped by paranoia and fear.

"I won't share a room," he shouted. "I won't!" He told us he had been mishandled in places like that—abused and raped by people who were supposed to care for him.

Late Friday afternoon, with nowhere else to turn, we hustled money from a church contact and got Ben a motel room for the weekend. We gave him our numbers, told him we'd check on him, and left him the only food he would eat: hot dogs "but no buns," fish "but no sardines," Pepsi "but no Coke," and Vienna sausages.

The next week we made dozens of calls. Surely seven competent members of our outreach team could find somewhere for him. But no one we called would touch Ben. He was either deemed "too sick" or "not sick enough" for their services. Finally, exasperated, one of our team members called Adult Protective Services, who sent a police officer out for an assessment. The officer talked to

Ben like he was a misbehaving dog. Afterward, the officer told us, "There's nothing we can do. He's not our problem until he's on the streets where we can pick him up for trespassing or worse."

Seven days with Ben and we were all spent. We had all taken shifts and knew that providing care for him was a full-time job. He required around-the-clock support, was often defiant, and needed constant pats, hugs, and attention. When he felt misunderstood or like we were forcing him to talk to "just one more person" about services, he raised his voice and pounded his fists on our desks.

After several more "no's" and closed doors, every last ounce of trust I had in the mental health system had been utterly drained. Jeannie called Robb, the nurse practitioner from the foot clinic, and he gave us our first "yes." Robb heard the desperation in Jeannie's voice and said he could give Ben a bed for the night at Room In The Inn's Guest House. He could sleep in the dining room by himself and have as many Pepsis as he wanted. I drove Ben to the Guest House, and after talking with Robb and thanking him profusely, I saw that Ben was holding hands by the entrance with an older resident named Eileen. She gave me a wink.

"I'm adopting Ben tonight," she beamed, "and we're gonna be just fine." Ben smiled like a child reunited with his long-lost mother.

The next day, I went back to take Ben to an appointment with a psychiatrist who ran a reputable boarding house for people with developmental disabilities and mental health issues. Eileen greeted me as I walked in, still holding Ben's hand.

"He did great last night," she said, beaming. I thanked her again and again. "I was just doing what was within me to do," she said. She hugged Ben goodbye and then vowed to pray for him every night. In response, Ben lifted his short, thick index finger and silently touched it to her nose. Eileen answered him by gently touching his nose. Ben smiled a wide, toothless grin.

To our utter amazement, Ben passed the psychiatrist's assessment and was offered a spot in the boarding house of our dreams.

But when we explained to him that he was in, he shouted a defiant "No!" Staying in the boarding house meant sharing a room. He wouldn't do it.

For the next few hours, we did everything we could to listen to Ben's concerns and reason with him. Ultimately, he refused, convinced he wouldn't be safe. He demanded that we take him to the nearest truck stop because he planned to hitch a ride with a nice trucker and go somewhere with better resources where he could start fresh.

Ben climbed into the passenger seat of my car. Jeannie dug through her bag and offered him a crumpled twenty, which he pocketed with care. I drove him to a truck stop and bought him one last Pepsi. The attendant noticed my puffy, bloodshot eyes and asked if I was okay.

"Allergies," I lied.

Did not our hearts break within us?

The Burial and Baptism of Kevin

Summer smoldered on as we worked ourselves raw. Jeannie and I met regularly with a growing council of Tent City residents intent on self-governance. Each council member represented a different area of the camp and headed up different tasks like security patrols and donation distribution. As Tent City grew, a mobile clinic started making rounds to the camp, a shower house was installed, and other volunteer groups came by regularly to offer sleeping bags, food, and worship services.

That summer, Teresa moved into an apartment, but Smurf stayed in the camp. He wasn't ready to live in a box with paper-thin walls and wasn't willing to give up his "critters, crosses, and freedom."

Amos House joined forces with Richard's community house and we began washing feet on the streets, hosting potlucks, and holding occasional contemplative services.

79

Jeannie and I both caught walking pneumonia from Kentucky, and while Kentucky hacked out his lungs on church stoops in the heat, I coughed on a couch in an air-conditioned room and watched Netflix. The disparities were stark.

That fall, I began my second year as an AmeriCorps VISTA at Park Center, and the weeks evaporated in a fog of meetings and fatigue. The winter came in fits and starts, but when the cold hit, it hit hard. Both extreme heat and extreme cold are deadly for our friends. While the summers suck the wind from outreach workers' sails, it's the winters that cause us to sink. It's the cold that settles into our bones, that wakes us up at night when we are safe and warm and our friends are losing fingers and toes. And that winter, like every winter, was marked by death.

Kevin, one of the residents of Tent City, was a quiet guy. None of us knew him well. On a frigid Wednesday night in mid-December, the temperature dipped into the low twenties. Bobby, Kevin's camp-mate, had settled into his tent, but Kevin huddled close to the fire for warmth on a plastic crate, sipping a forty of beer. Gradually, he lost consciousness. Perhaps it was the alcohol. Perhaps it was the exhaustion of survival. Perhaps it was the fumes rising from the creosote-treated timber he was burning. But at some point during the night, he fell into the fire and caught. No one ever heard him scream. He only crackled and popped.

The next morning, Bobby found what was left of Kevin and the crate that was melted to him. The investigators came and removed what they could, leaving a ghastly carbon imprint where he had lain. Pieces of Kevin remained among the ashes and stuck to the remnants of his scratchy gray blanket. Jeannie rushed to the camp as soon as she heard the news. With tenderness and care, she helped Bobby gather the charred remains of Kevin in the blanket.

Bobby told Jeannie that Kevin wanted to be "buried at sea" even though he couldn't swim. "Since he'd never been baptized," said Bobby, "he wanted his burial to serve as his baptism."

So that bitter, frosty morning, Jeannie, Bobby, and a few others carried what was left of Kevin down to the Cumberland River. The dawning city hushed and held her breath as if she knew the horrors that had taken place. In the shadow of the bridge high overhead, distant tires hummed on pavement. As commuters carried on, a handful of mourners granted Kevin's last request for a burial at sea.

"I baptize you in the name of the Father, the Son, and the Holy Spirit," said Bobby.

And our hearts broke and burned.

6

WILDERNESS

KEVIN DIED, and the winter wore on.

First it was snow. Then ice. Hundreds of tons of salt and brine were sprayed over streets, and fifty water mains shattered underground. I went out with other outreach workers in four-wheel-drive SUVs crammed with coats, sleeping bags, emergency blankets, thermals, and propane. We hiked miles down icy train tracks to reach outlying camps. We searched alleys and underpasses for people who needed to come in. We found a kind, wiry woman wrapped in layers of cardboard and plastic. A man with a gray, bulbous nose in sky-blue hospital clothes wandering a honky-tonk ghost town. Couples huddling in snow-laden tents hours after the last of their propane evaporated into thin, bitter air. Dozens more. How many did we miss?

We drove them to the makeshift shelter we had opened where blankets draped over cots and overflow pallets covered the church floor. After our rounds, I stayed overnight as an innkeeper. I pulled a thin blanket over myself on the cold linoleum, so tired I was dizzy. The smell of unwashed bodies and urine washed over me.

Then lion-loud snoring, coughing, and hacking. Sighs and muffled night shouts.

Despite my exhaustion, I couldn't sleep. How many people did I miss? I made a list in my head of all the underpasses and campsites I couldn't reach. I felt guilt. Grief. A terrible knowing that my exhaustion paled in comparison to that of everyone else in the room, everyone who was still outside.

Feelings of loss and responsibility piled on top of me, weighing me down. I knew Andrew was at home—worried. He knew the toll winters took on me, on our team, on our friends on the streets. After texting him goodnight, I managed to doze off. Sometime later, a lengthening light moved across the fellowship hall, and I heard gurgling from pots percolating in the kitchen followed by the smell of coffee. Processed blueberry bars were served for breakfast. I folded up my blanket, knowing later that night we would do it all again.

Shelf Life

"You know, the shelf life of an outreach worker is two to three years," said my friend matter-of-factly. I argued with him, listed all the people I knew who outlasted that. But nearly every name I offered, he debunked. Almost all had shifted roles after two to three years. In a couple years, he too would leave his outreach work with youth. I was now nearly two years in myself and close to breaking. How much more time did I have?

That Sunday at Otter Creek, a passage from Matthew was read from the pulpit. "Take my yoke upon you. . . . For my yoke is easy and my burden is light" (11:29–30).

My exhaustion morphed into anger that boiled in me from the padded pews.

Easy? I thought. *Light? How could Jesus say that? What a lie.*

There were always more calls, texts, and emails than I could answer, always more needs than I could meet. People were upset

84

when I didn't get back to them quickly enough. I was trapped in the tension between telling myself that the responsibility for others didn't rest solely on my shoulders and knowing that many situations depended on my response. John wanted to hurt himself and needed to talk. Mary was in the hospital and needed an advocate. Alan would be evicted if I didn't get him the check that was mailed to our office. Sarah and her daughter needed twenty dollars or their water would be turned off. Joe was trying to mediate a fight at the camp and needed help.

I woke in the middle of the night with work dreams—people hurting, people in need. The mornings were the worst. As I drove to work, my chest tightened, prickled, caved. My heart was a flock of blackbirds beating against a locked and windowless room. Everything spiraled out of control, and when the birds burst out, an emptiness crawled inside, making my heart its den.

> *I was trapped in the tension between telling myself that the responsibility for others didn't rest solely on my shoulders and knowing that many situations depended on my response.*

For the first time in my life, I couldn't pray. The words and thoughts withered and hardened like a neglected houseplant no rain could reach. I felt salty, angry, abandoned. My roots reached for the smallest drop only to find bone-dry soil, clay walls caging me in. A feeling beyond exhaustion, beyond despair—a kind of wilderness—began to take root.

That spring, my bad ankle flared up. It was like it was buckling under the weight of all the burdens I was carrying. "Tenosynovitis," said the doctor—inflammation around a tendon. I would have to do special exercises every morning and night, use oral and topical anti-inflammatories, wear a carbon-fiber footplate, and spend weeks on crutches.

Night after night, I came home bereft. I longed to be held, but like a mimosa plant whose leaves retract at the slightest touch, I withdrew, folded inward.

Andrew felt helpless. He encouraged me to rest, but I kept going. Like my work, his work with *The Contributor* was focused on people who were struggling to survive without housing. But while he also felt the heaviness of the work, the nature of outreach was different, and the way I buckled beneath its weight affected him too.

I imagined going back in time to our wedding—brick red church, eggshell colored dress, the radiant faces of friends and family—to give Andrew full disclosure.

I need you to know what you're getting into with me, I imagined saying. *I will come home from work utterly hollowed out with no space for you. I will melt into sobs on the couch while you're left wondering what to do, how to help, needing things from me I cannot give.*

I should have told him I would stare for hours into the dark edge of our living room where the gray-blue wall met the white speckled ceiling. *I know you need me to be your friend, your partner, your lover*, I continued in my mind, *and not a wife with her brain scrambled to sulfur like eggs too long in the skillet.*

I should have told him I was sorry. He deserved better.

Would he still have married me if he knew how it would be?

How long could we sustain this?

Rest

As Holy Week approached, I took to crutches. Andrew and I were set to spend Good Friday and Holy Saturday on the streets. As the Citywide Stations of the Cross event approached, I borrowed a wheelchair from our donation room. That night, our group huddled together and slept on the concrete stoop of a downtown church. The next morning, we were drenched by an unexpected downpour and made our way to the Jefferson Street Bridge for lunch, sloshing in wet tennis shoes. Clear, fluid-filled blisters bloomed on my palms from the wheelchair, so members of our group took turns pushing me on bumpy, treacherous, partially accessible sidewalks. When we arrived, my friend who was a one-legged vet rolled up to me in his chair, showed me the hilly calluses on his hands, and told me the best route back downtown.

Then, I felt someone tap my shoulder.

"Lindsey, is that you?"

I turned around to see a tall, tan, handsome man with cedar hair pulled back in a ponytail.

"Kentucky?!" I shouted, and he leaned down for a hug. For nearly a year, our team had wondered about him. Was he dead? In jail? Pushing his cart of mouthwash or sleeping on church stoops in some distant city? After nearly forty days of detox and treatment at the VA, we lost touch and couldn't get any information about where he had gone.

"I lost your number," Kentucky said. "I think about y'all all the time." He stood upright, gleaming with a new set of dentures. He was staying in a halfway house. Healthy. Sober. Resurrected.

"You and Jeannie said we'd celebrate and that y'all'd take me out to dinner when I was sobered-up and housed," he said.

I smiled. "That offer still stands," I said, scribbling my number on a napkin.

We caught up until it was time for my group to go. With another hug and a "call me—for real," we said goodbye.

I texted Jeannie and other members of our team. Everyone was elated. But the days stretched into weeks, the weeks into months, and still no call.

We never saw or heard from Kentucky again. In less than a year, he would be dead. The rumor was that he relapsed, hit the streets, died under that very bridge. One lady said it was liver failure. Another said he was robbed and beaten.

Another verse from the same passage in Matthew surfaced in me. "Come to me, all you who are weary and burdened, and I will give you rest" (Matt. 11:28).

Rest? I thought. *Yeah right.*

The Rain Came Down

May in Nashville is a muggy, hapless month. That April, the un-seasonally arid earth prayed for respite, and the dawning of May answered with mountains of pregnant smoky-blue clouds that settled low over the region. Then, as if a lever had been pulled from above, the clouds let loose an endless fury. A record 13.5 inches of rain came down in thirty-six hours. Fearing a dam would give way, the Army Corps of Engineers released over five billion gal-lons of frothy, roiling water into the Cumberland River. Streams bloated into rivers, rivers expanded into lakes. Ponds of brown water engulfed entire neighborhoods and parking lots. Roads, bridges, and whole sections of interstate disappeared. A portable building floated down a section of flooded interstate. When all was said and done, eleven people in the Nashville area had died and more than ten thousand were displaced.

I dialed a church leader who was on his way to evacuate Tent City residents. Water had crept into tents, going from puddle-deep to knee-deep in a matter of minutes. It climbed over bee-kissed thistles and drowned the vines of cherry tomatoes Vegas planted by the fence. It rose around the port-o-potties and shower house and sunset-colored trumpet vines that snaked up interstate pillars. Most people lost everything. When the Cumberland was at its highest, the only thing visible in Tent City was the shingled roof of Cowboy's shanty that held a cluster of his cats hanging off one edge and a tangle of rats hanging off the other.[1]

Of the hundred and forty Tent City residents, seventy came to the Red Cross shelter with their pets, thirty stayed in local churches, and the rest, like Smurf, doubled up with friends or moved to higher ground. As the floodwaters receded, city leaders declared Tent City "condemned" as a health and safety hazard rather than merely "contaminated." This designation excluded it from receiving public assistance for clean-up and prohibited the residents from going back to the only home they had. If they did, they would be cited or arrested.

Before the flood, there was a clear understanding that Tent City would eventually have to move from its current site. The Tennessee Department of Transportation was set to begin construction on the bridges above the camp later that November, so in February, the Homelessness Commission had formed two subcommittees to address the situation: a site relocation committee and a model committee. Jeannie and I were on the latter.

Despite regular meetings, both committees fell silent after the flood. It was as if the problem of Tent City was now swept away— out of sight, out of mind. Like Pilate, the city officials washed their hands of responsibility. We started looking for land we could use when the Red Cross shelter closed. Charlie helped us draft a resolution that we presented to the Homelessness Commission on May 7, petitioning them to request a temporary variance of codes and zoning regulations once land was located. We were told our efforts would be supported, but we received no solid commitments. Shortly thereafter, as the closing of the shelter drew near, members of the commission stopped returning our calls and excluded us from planning meetings.

A representative from Otter Creek took the lead on searching for land. Jeannie and I joined with other outreach workers and volunteers to fill out FEMA claims and housing paperwork. The city's housing authority was offering Section 8 housing vouchers to flood victims, but in order to qualify, people had to make it through background checks and have their IDs, social security cards, birth certificates, and income verifications. Receiving an out-of-state birth certificate, however, could take up to eight weeks, and for those who were approved, we would still have to find apartments that accepted the vouchers. The pressures piled on, and we needed all the help we could get. One of the volunteers who joined us was Brett, a tall, Kentucky-raised sophomore at Lipscomb with long blond hair. Brett was in a perpetual state of existential angst and had been following Jeannie around for months, trying to figure out his life and faith. He fit right in.

In the evenings, we emailed and posted on social media to collect clothing, camping supplies, and volunteers. A youth group from out of state drove a trailer packed with tents to Otter Creek. Another group brought dozens of sleeping bags and tarps. And then, an email landed in my inbox. It was from Ingrid, a thirty-something firebrand Methodist who had just quit her comfortable job because she felt like she was wasting God's time. "I just got tired of pulling my hair out from working with institutions that were unwilling to risk and imagine," she told me. She was searching for a way to be useful in flood relief efforts and had met Jeannie and me at a church meeting that spring. "I'm at your disposal," she wrote. From then on, she was by our side. We were a ragtag team, intent on doing everything we could for our friends.

The Promise and the Promised Land

Two weeks after Tent City residents moved their lives into a crowded gymnasium with hundreds of other flood victims, the Red Cross announced their closing date: May 18.

"Where are we gonna go?" asked dozens of displaced residents at a meeting among the cots.

"We don't have an answer for that yet," we told them, "but we're working on it."

"And we can promise this," I added, "whatever happens, we're not going to abandon you."

"Right," said Jeannie, "even if it means we all camp on the lawn in front of city hall and get arrested together. We're in this with you, by your side."

We had no idea how that promise would wring us out. But we made it. We meant it. And we would do it all over again.

The day the shelter closed was chaos. Scattered cots. Packed bags. Barking pit bulls on leashes. Couples with no idea where they would go. A handful of Tent City folks had already received vouchers or FEMA money and moved on. The Homelessness Commission scrounged up a handful of one-week hotel vouchers, distributed them somewhat randomly, and bused folks out to a cheap hotel. Jeannie, Brett, Ingrid, and I brought our cars to the shelter, and a leader from Otter Creek brought the church van. Our fifty-or-so friends with nowhere to go piled in and we drove to Otter Creek, where volunteers provided lunch.

As people ate, we went table to table, meeting with each person to make a plan while Ingrid called churches. We joked that because she grew up with a father who was a well-known Methodist minister, went to Wesley Theological Seminary, and had worked for the United Methodist Church, she was in the "Methodist Mafia." We still didn't have land, but there were a couple leads, and within a few hours, Ingrid had two churches who were willing to open their doors for another week. Those who couldn't afford hotels moved into the churches, and Ingrid coordinated food, supplies, and transportation.

We kept pushing city officials to help us, but only our Otter Creek representative—a white male minister—was invited to their meetings. The doors were closed to me, Jeannie, Ingrid, Brett, and former Tent City residents. The city was still reeling, and we had exhausted our resources.

Then, miraculously, a week and a half after hearing "no" everywhere we turned, we received a call back from one of the landowners we contacted. The call was from the millionaire owner of a local car dealership, who was also a member at Otter Creek. He explained that he had a 124-acre tract of land in Antioch that wasn't being used. "They're flood victims too," he said. "Sounds like the right thing to do."

The landowner agreed to lease the property to Amos House for one dollar for ninety days and to consider an extension if needed. We would get liability waivers and community rules signed by residents, rent a dumpster and a couple port-o-potties for the site, and lean on a religious land-use law called RLUIPA—the Religious Land Use and Institutionalized Persons Act. This law stated that people who use land for religious purposes can't be "substantially burdened" by zoning laws. It felt like we were about to enter the Promised Land after wandering in the wilderness. In the end, twenty-eight people decided to move to the property, and the rest resettled in smaller camps across the city. We staked out a two-acre patch of land off a dirt road in a neighborhood in Antioch called Hickory Hollow. Waist-high grass swayed in the late-May breeze beneath the omniscient glare of sun that tried to warn us away. A tree line provided some shade, but the mosquitoes and flies were relentless. The residents picked their spots and we joined tent poles together, pushed them through long, thin nylon sleeves, and anchored them into the dirt. It wasn't perfect, but it was land—a temporary reprieve that kept our friends safe and together until housing or FEMA money came through or we found another spot.

As soon as the word spread about the resettlement, camera teams and reporters swarmed the scene. When the news stories aired, our dream of reprieve vanished. Outraged Antioch residents caught an infectious case of NIMBYism—Not in My Back Yard—and held a meeting to organize opposition. The council member who was running for reelection tried to get an injunction to kick us off the property, which sent Metro codes and the health department over for inspections. When the injunction was delayed, the council member told the landowner that if he didn't evict the residents, he wouldn't help rezone his land. Luckily, the landowner was too rich and powerful to care. Then, Homelessness Commission leaders who had been supportive of our efforts withdrew support. "It's too political," they said. They refused to meet with us, saying that their executive board told them to stay out of it.

Resistance to "the new Tent City" mounted in Antioch and added business owners and pastors to its ranks who claimed to care for people who were unhoused but didn't want our friends to contribute to the "downfall" of their area. The vitriol spewed online and in news stories was so disturbing that we held a workshop for Tent City residents on how to respond to hate speech and avoid violence. We were terrified and worried that angry, armed Antioch residents would storm the camp.

Nine days after we moved to the land, a public meeting was held at Living Word Community Church. Some camp residents decided to stay at the camp and keep watch in case of any funny business.

Andrew had been helping to document the unfolding events in *The Contributor* and came with me to the meeting. On our way, we picked up Vegas, who was on the governing council at Tent City, and a six-foot-five lumberjack of a man named Dave. Dave always wore a flannel shirt tucked into fitted jeans tied off with a belt, even in the heat of summer. Tonight was no different. He had just lobbed the sleeves off his shirt so his long, tan, wiry-muscle arms hung through. When we pulled up, we had to circle the parking lot to find an empty spot. The church was bustling, overflowing like Easter Sunday. We found a few seats together several rows from the front.

"I'm gonna stand in the back," said Dave, tucking a Pall Mall behind his ear. "I gotta pace for this one."

As the meeting began, every pew was packed, and news cameras, standers, and pacers like Dave lined the walls. Jeannie was wearing her "Jesus was homeless" t-shirt. I nervously struck up a conversation with a church member from Antioch in front of me. She seemed nice and handed me her card. When she realized I was "with them," however, she scowled. "I need my card back," she said through squinted eyes and lips pushed tight.

The three-hour meeting was moderated by the council member. It featured a rousing monologue by Pastor Rodney Beard, an interview in which Jeannie and our Otter Creek representative were essentially grilled before a seething audience, and a scathing stream of public comments. This was Beard's home church, and he knew how to work a crowd. He started off with a low, reasonable pitch saying he was "for the homeless." But then his pitch heightened, his pace quickened, and his intensity built until the crowd was galvanized.

"How many of you have heard of 'Hickory Harlem'?" he asked, referring to the Hickory Hollow neighborhood in Antioch where the camp was located. "We are trying to bring businesses and schools to Antioch!" he shouted. He bellowed on about how they were being dumped on, as if we were bringing trash and not human beings who found themselves displaced by what people were calling the thousand-year flood.

"No more bringing anything to Antioch that is not positive!" he yelled from the pulpit. "The gates of Antioch's charity are closed!"[2] To this the crowd erupted in applause and amens, with people rising to their feet as if an electric shock had just run across the floor. From the stage, Jeannie looked visibly shaken.

The gates of charity are closed?

By the public comment section, I was all nerves. My face flushed, and I was barely able to process what was unfolding.

"We asked the Lord," said one Antioch resident, "and the Lord said we shouldn't give them anything."

"We can't help what's going on in the world," said another, "this isn't our problem. You've forced charity down our throats!"

"We are not a dumping ground," the voices continued.

"This is bad for business."

"I'm a Christian, but . . ."

"I'm a Christian, but . . ."

Vegas leaned over to me. "I see why y'all trained us in nonviolence."

It was not lost on us that we were sitting in Living Word Community Church. Rather than seeing the Word take on flesh, however, we witnessed a warped and idolatrous version of the gospel that twisted good news for the poor into a

94

health and wealth gospel. Instead of compassion, we were offered injunctions. Instead of hospitality, we faced hostility. Instead of upholding the value of human life, we saw property values exalted. It was what Jeannie later called "the gospel of counterfeit Christendom."[3]

Even now, years later, it's tempting not to paint the council member, pastor, and other members of Living Word as villains. But that's not the whole story. Residents of Antioch claimed a long history of divestment—of city money that failed to reach their schools, community centers, and sidewalks the way it reached other areas of town. Living Word was predominantly Black, and even though Tent City was diverse, our Otter Creek representative, Jeannie, Ingrid, Brett, and I were all white. These issues are layered and complex—as things often are. Several times throughout the public meeting, Antioch residents, often Black, asked why we hadn't taken Tent City residents to camp at the predominantly white, wealthy Otter Creek Church.

"It's not on the bus line," the Otter Creek representative countered. The critics shook their heads in dismay.

Here's the thing. Capitalism and white supremacy are, as Dorothy Day would say, "filthy rotten systems." Black residents of Antioch were already starting off behind many white Nashvillians whose families had been building wealth for decades—if not centuries—and whose ancestors had never faced the brutal realities of slavery, the Jim Crow South, and redlining.[4] One of the surest ways for middle-income Americans to increase wealth is to build equity through homeownership. That equity is swayed by property values, and while a number of factors affect those values, people often fear that if poorer folks move into their neighborhood, everything will tank. Too often, NIMBYism ensues, pitting the once-poor against the still-poor.

To be clear, I'm not saying the council member and Antioch pastor were right. I'm saying that these men and many church members allowed themselves to be driven by fear, by stereotypes, and by a warped version of the gospel. But if that was true of Living Word, it was also true of city officials who failed to show. It was true as well of all the churches who locked their doors, put up "no trespassing" signs, and turned away our friends, the living Christ.

Not long after the meeting, city officials served the camp an eviction notice. We were in violation of the city's no-camping ordinance, with or without religious land-use laws. We would have to be off the property forty days after we had settled.

With threadbare spirits, we continued our search for another site. The waiting lists for housing were still long, and the couples and pet owners couldn't access traditional shelters. Finally, just days before we were set to leave Antioch, Ingrid and her Methodist Mafia connections came through. The pastor of Hobson United Methodist Church gave us permission to use their five-bedroom parsonage for ninety days. All we had to do was pay utilities.

Out of the twenty-eight campers on the land, a few got housing, a few got FEMA money, and a few decided to move to other camps. We moved the remaining seventeen people into what we would call "Hobson House"—a two-story brick parsonage with a generous front porch. It was tucked away in a homey residential neighborhood in East Nashville on the bus line. It was a land flowing with possibilities and hope—a roof, real showers, real plumbing, air conditioning, and a full kitchen.

Hobson House quickly became an intentional community where the residents split the utilities, established community rules, and held weekly meetings where everyone went around and shared their "highs and lows." They kept up with chores, mowed the lawn, worked through their conflicts nonviolently (for the most part), and maintained a drug-free environment (also for the most part). We participated in the daily life and rhythms of Hobson House, and Andrew joined me for shifts where we spent the night as innkeepers. It wasn't all daisies and roses, but there was air conditioning in the summer, heat in the winter, and a sense of togetherness.

As the summer drew to a close, Jeannie and I both prepared
to leave Park Center. I was planning to start graduate school in
the fall, and she planned to teach at a local college and get more
involved with prison chaplaincy. For the better part of a year, we
had both been taking heat for our activism in the community. I
had been pulled aside by my boss's boss because of comments I
made at a Homelessness Commission meeting that were critical
of the director's management of funds. Someone on the executive board had threatened to pull some of Park Center's funding
if Jeannie and I kept speaking out. "Don't they know they are
biting the hand that feeds them?" the board member said. While
we both were committed to the work we were doing, we needed
to find another vehicle in which to do it.

Running

Three-and-a-half months after the flood, Andrew and I enrolled
in graduate courses at Vanderbilt Divinity School. We were both
drawn to theology but had different goals. He was interested in
teaching and writing. I was looking for space to process what I had
experienced on the streets. I wanted to find someone to help me
figure out how to do this work sustainably—not just for a couple
years but for the long haul. Perhaps my outreach friend was right
about his "shelf-life theory." Outreach had already taken a heavy
toll on my marriage, my body, my mind, and my spirit, but it
wasn't just a job to me. It was a vocation.

My plan for the fall semester was that I would stay involved with
Hobson House, plunge myself into my studies, and babysit to pay
the bills. Babysitting felt like a kind of professional regression, but
I got over that quickly. It had flexible hours and paid closer to a
living wage than anything else I could find, and I loved the kids.
When I began to be assigned four hundred to five hundred pages
of reading a week on top of written assignments, however, the intensity of graduate studies began to sink in. During a particularly

heavy week, I strained my eyes so badly a blood vessel burst, leaving a cloud of inky red in my right eye for days.

"I just feel off," I told Andrew several weeks in. The ground beneath my feet felt as if it were physically shifting.

One of my classes that fall was a pastoral care class with Dr. Barbara McClure. Dr. McClure had a wavy angled bob the color of sunlit grain and wore what I thought of as scientist glasses. She was the first person I had ever heard make a distinction between being responsible *for* others and responsible *to* them. During my work at Park Center, I had often struggled with the idea of responsibility.

Are we our sibling's keeper? I asked myself. *Absolutely*, came the response. *Are we to run our bodies into a heap of sobs by canvassing the entire city in winter when our friends are at risk of freezing to death?* I asked. *You bet.*

But instead of understanding this as a collective responsibility—one shouldered together by a community—I understood it as an individual one. If this was the case, the burden was heavy indeed. Dorothy Day was of little help to me here because of her emphasis on taking personal responsibility for the injustice and suffering in the world—something that resonated with me but could also be problematic if the weight of responsibility was shifted too far away from unjust systems.

"If you take responsibility *for* someone," explained Dr. McClure, "you end up taking on their anxieties and possibly even enabling them. This can sometimes look like 'overfunctioning.'" I thought of my grandmother and grandfather and the way they coddled some of my family members who struggled with severe mental health and addiction issues, who lied and stole from them, and who desperately needed professional help. My grandparents' overfunctioning and codependency allowed these family members to underfunction. I knew something about this from my own work as well. "When you are responsible *to* them, however," continued Dr. McClure, "you help them manage their own anxieties, solve their own problems."

Being responsible *for* someone was akin to carrying them. Being responsible *to* someone meant walking beside them.

Later that day in class, we had breakout groups, and I landed in Dr. McClure's group. When it was my turn to share, I spoke about how difficult the summer was. About how after the flood I worked more than seventy hours a week and had trouble sleeping. I felt like I was wandering through an emotional wilderness and had tense muscles, a constricting chest, fatigue, and a sense of dread, anger, or apathy whenever my phone rang. After I finished, Dr. McClure let the silence linger and then leaned in.

"All that work," she said, "and with such consequences. It makes me wonder. In all of your busy-ness, what were you running from?"

Her question caused me to recoil back in my chair.

What was I running from?

I was offended. My face flushed. "I wasn't running from any-thing," I said, a little too defensively. "I had a good childhood. I'm a healthy person. I was just doing what needed to be done."

She raised her eyebrows, pushed her scientist glasses back on her nose, and let the silence hold. She didn't push me any further; she just leaned back and asked who wanted to share next. She knew she had done her work.

Her question lingered heavy on my mind and heart. It would be several years before I discovered an answer.

A Place at the Table

One weekend in late September, as sprays of goldenrod lit the roadside, our Otter Creek representative, Jeannie, Ingrid, Brett, and I drove to Normandy, Tennessee, for a retreat at a bed and breakfast managed by Ingrid's parents. We hadn't truly caught our breath together since the flood. We had weekly dinners at Ingrid's place, sometimes starting as late as nine in the evening, but we needed to unplug from ceaseless calls and requests that vied for our attention.

Something had been born out of the diesel-soaked floodwaters, and we needed to figure out what it was. Park Center was no longer a base for our outreach work, and neither was Otter Creek. We wanted to keep Amos House what it was—small, organic, low to the ground. But there was a need for something more, something else. By then, the Power Project had imploded, leaving a gaping hole in the world of homeless advocacy and organizing. There were secular nonprofits doing outreach, but they couldn't mobilize faith communities or work toward more holistic healing. What was needed in Nashville was more than charity, more than case management, more than a model to "reintegrate people back into society" as some nonprofits postured. When we looked around us, we saw a fractured society that propped up personal gain and whiteness, put property rights over human rights, and discarded our friends into the living hells of missions, jails, streets, and slums.

That night, the expansive, wood-paneled New Mexico–style living room opened its arms to us. We sunk into cloudlike couches and wrapped ourselves in afghans. The evening's air carried the tease of fall, and a couple bottles of pinot noir warmed us from the inside out. It was glorious. For hours, we lost ourselves in conversation.

What were we doing? What were the needs? What was our vision?

In the end, we decided that something new already existed, and we needed to name it. Our first choice, "Open Door," was already taken, so we decided on "Open Table"—not to be confused with the dinner reservation company. Oh, hindsight. Most of us were theologically trained, so table imagery struck a deep chord. We thought of the "messianic banquets" in Isaiah and Matthew and Luke. We thought of breaking bread and the magic that happened over shared meals. We wanted to create an environment of radical welcome, something that would disrupt the table politics of the status quo.

As we talked, Jeannie spoke about the incarnation of Jesus as a radical act of solidarity. Brett talked about how cool it was that he, at twenty years old, was drinking wine. Ingrid mentioned a song called "A Place at the Table" that Methodists love. I told them about a Bill Moyers quote I had come across years before. "Faith-based charity provides crumbs from the table," Moyers said. "Faith-based justice offers a place at the table."[5] It was settled.

When we got back to Nashville, we found an attorney to start the process of registering Open Table Nashville as an interfaith 501(c)(3) nonprofit. The mission statement would come later, but we knew we were creating an entity where disrupting systems that perpetuate injustice was as important as accompanying people on the journey toward housing, healing, and hope. We would build a grassroots funding base with private funds through relationships so we wouldn't be beholden to government funding or any single funder. At that point, we had no funding, no strategic plan, and no office space. It would be three years until I was able to be paid, but it didn't matter. We had the trust of our friends on the streets and a spark of something fierce. And we had each other.

The Last Shall Be First

After our lease was extended at Hobson House, the following November Stacey and Bama, two of the residents, were married at the old Tent City. Jeannie officiated in shiny black knee-high combat boots. "My one wish," said Stacey as we were planning, "is that everyone who's homeless and hungry can get a warm meal." So after the service a feast was served. Ingrid went through the line, ushering everyone who was unhoused to the front.

"The last shall be first!" she said to me and winked.

That winter brought five snowfalls—a surprising amount for a southern city like ours—and each brought the need for several nights of emergency shelters. When city officials dragged their feet about opening overflow shelters, Ingrid pleaded with the minister at

Hobson to let us utilize the fellowship hall, and he obliged. One night as I was canvassing the brine-soaked streets of downtown, I saw a man wearing a tattered jacket who looked lost. His scraggly gray beard hung low, and as he shuffled, his head was bowed toward the ground like a monk in prayer. I pulled up and we exchanged names.

"Do you need a place to stay?" I asked. Frank nodded but refused go to the Nashville Rescue Mission. "This is different," I told him. As he climbed in my car, I saw a hospital bracelet around his wrist. He managed to mutter that he had been in the hospital for seven days and was discharged in the snow.

When we arrived at the fellowship hall, I helped Frank hobble over to a cot, and Stacey brought him a cup of coffee. We asked him some basic orienting questions—Do you know where you are? What day of the week is it? Who is the president?—and then asked how his feet were doing. He leaned down to remove his shoes and hospital socks. Bandages peeked out, oozing with yellow fluid, and a pungent smell stung our noses.

"Frostbite," he murmured.

How was he discharged like this? I thought.

Frank pulled a folded stack of discharge papers from his jacket and handed them to Jeannie. There were several prescriptions he needed, so Jeannie left to get them filled. Then he began to scratch his left forearm through his jacket.

"What's going on, honey?" asked Stacey. "Let me take a look." She gently pulled up his sleeve to see that an IV catheter was still taped down and lodged in his forearm. Frank wanted it out.

Stacey was trained in first aid and wound care and knew how to safely remove catheters. She got the medical supplies, slipped on blue latex gloves, gently removed the catheter, and cleaned and dressed the area.

"That feel better, hon?" she asked. Frank nodded. "Now let's take a look at those feet."

After tending Frank, Stacey walked next door to Hobson House. She came back carrying a stack of extra pajama pants and long-sleeve shirts and began to hand them out to the women. As she walked by me, I smiled and she hip-bumped me.

"I don't forget where I come from," she said.

Bama was helping with the cots and blankets, and when he noticed we didn't have a sweatshirt large enough for Frank, he pulled off his hoodie and brought it over.

"Here ya go, sir," he said without thinking twice.

Stacey and Bama's moving display of hospitality and solidarity touched me deeply, but it no longer surprised me. I had come to see that it was often our friends with the least who were willing to give the most.

Spinning

Between helping with Hobson House and the emergency shelters, I was still going to grad school and babysitting. I also couldn't shake the feeling of being "off," and I was still struggling with anxiety. For over a year, I'd been doing speaking gigs whenever I was asked, mostly with Sunday school classes and student groups. Speaking in public was beginning to feel more natural, but on days where my anxiety was heightened, my nerves frayed and my confidence waned.

My friend who was a professor at Lipscomb asked me to speak to his class at the Tennessee Prison for Women one night. Half the students were traditional Lipscomb students and half were incarcerated at the prison. I had spoken to his class before and nailed it, but this night felt different. It had been a terrible week. I had my speaking notes but had to leave my bottle of water in the car. As I locked the doors, I could feel my chest constricting. I could feel a tightness in my jaw, a shakiness in my hands.

We passed through razor-wire fences, metal detectors, and several steel doors to reach the classroom. The windowless concrete room was chilly. As we pulled the chair-desks into a large circle, they screeched across the floor. When the professor introduced me, the walls began closing in. He turned it over to me, and within a few minutes I was stumbling over my words. Every ounce of moisture drained from my mouth. It was desert-dry. My tongue felt swollen and stiff. The room fell silent. Students looked down at their notebooks, fumbled with their pens. There was no water anywhere.

To this day, I have no idea how the class ended. It was as if I had blacked out.

When I got to my car, I gulped down water, and on the drive home, a hot shame I couldn't shake welled up from my belly to my heart to my head.

The "off" feeling took on a new edge in March. One morning, I was studying at a coffee shop when my phone buzzed. It was one of the outreach leaders from Otter Creek. I stepped into the crisp March air and answered his call.

"Lindsey, we need to talk," he said. There was no emotion in his voice. He sounded eerily calm, as if he were reading a script. "I'm going to be stepping down from Open Table."

My heart quickened as the trapped birds tore their wings against my chest. He explained that he would be shifting roles, "effective immediately."

"Don't you think we should have a board meeting to discuss the transition?" I asked.

"I'm not going to be able to do that," he said. He explained that because I was an Otter Creek member, I would be his liaison to Open Table. Tears stung my eyes. How would we do this without his help and connections, without the formal support from Otter Creek's outreach ministry?

I sat stunned on the sidewalk with my hand cupped over my mouth. Jeannie was at the prison, so after several minutes, I called Ingrid. When she picked up, we were both silent and then started to sob. "Where are you?" I asked.

"Home," she said.

"Can I come over?"

"Of course."

I packed up my books, and we spent the next several hours talking and crying on her couch, trying to figure out how to navigate what felt like an abandonment, a betrayal, a new wilderness.

Three days later, I started spinning—"It's vertigo," said the student health nurse—and the whole world turned on its end.

7

EMERGENCE

I BURROWED INTO THE COUCH beside Andrew and leaned into him, eyes locked into news footage from Cairo. We were speechless. A month after a Tunisian fruit vendor burned himself alive in an act of desperation against government corruption, mass protests forced Tunisia's president out of the country. Uprisings were sparked across the Middle East and North Africa. The Arab Spring was just beginning in 2011, sending flares of resistance throughout the world. In Egypt, millions mobilized to demand the overthrow of President Hosni Mubarak, a dictator whose thirty-year rule allowed for widespread corruption and poverty to fester.

The Egyptian revolution was unfolding on a global stage, and we couldn't pull ourselves away. The images smoldered in my mind. Makeshift barricades separating tanks from children. Clouds of tear gas drifting through the streets. Police batons. Government water canons and live rounds fired into crowds. Aerial shots of Tahrir Square with a circle of plastic tents in the center surrounded by tens of thousands of people. Hundreds of Muslims facing east, bent in Friday prayer, protected by a circle of Egyptian Christians holding hands. Chants ringing out, some in English—"Muslim,

Christian, doesn't matter, we're all in this boat together!" Thousands injured and arrested. Hundreds dead.

"If we were there," I said to Andrew, "I hope we'd be out on the streets with them." As we watched the latest news reports, I tried to imagine the risks the protesters were taking, the violence they faced, the loss they endured, the collective hope that pulsed through their veins. Later that summer, protests would ignite in cities like Rome, London, Tokyo, Berlin, and Barcelona to denounce corruption, greed, and political and economic systems the prioritized profit over the well-being of people.

If sparks were to ignite here, where would our convictions and commitments take us?

Belonging

April in Nashville is pure magic. The sunlit yellow of forsythias and the stunning white of dogwoods and Bradford pears have come and gone. The fuchsia blooms of redbuds reign. Seeing the world come alive in spring brought me back to myself. I was still spinning but inching toward steadier ground. I pulled my 4Runner up to the Drake Motel just south of downtown. A faded sign out front read, "Stay where the stars stay," but it had been decades since anyone with wealth or fame had stayed within their walls.

"Hey, Ken, it's me!" I said as I knocked on the door.

I could hear Ken rustling around inside but didn't expect a response. Ken had lost his ability to talk and walk due to a cancerous brain tumor growing against his spinal cord. After a couple minutes, he opened the door and cigarette smoke billowed out.

"You ready for this?" I asked.

Ken held both thumbs up toward me and smiled with his lips twisting to the left like always. The silver hoop earring in his left ear glinted in the light and a faded camo hat covered his thick, sandy-brown mullet pulled neatly into a ponytail. With wiry arms, he wheeled himself over to my car and lifted his eighty-five-pound body into the passenger seat. I folded up his forty-pound chair and loaded it into the back—a task I now aced with impressive ease.

"Damn, girl!" said one of Ken's neighbors as I hoisted the chair up and in.

"I'm stronger than I look!" I joked.

Ken was set to be the guest speaker at our Wednesday night Vespers service at Otter Creek. Instead of speaking, his answers to pre-asked questions would scroll across the screen.

I would tell the audience that on a sweltering day the summer before, I met Ken at the park in front of the downtown library. He rolled up to me and held up a piece of paper with one word scribbled across it in all caps: "HELP." We went over to the shade and as I asked him questions, he scribbled answers on his notepad. Ken was forty-seven years old with sun-creased skin and coastal blue eyes. He had been on the streets on and off since he was fourteen. He didn't have his ID, birth certificate, or social security card. He received disability benefits, but his debit card from Chase Bank wasn't working. He couldn't call customer service because he couldn't speak, and there were no Chase banks in Nashville. Ken was advocating for himself but needed someone to advocate with him. I said "Yes," and we began putting the pieces of his life back together. We communicated through email until he got a phone and got his documents and his bank card turned back on. Over the course of several weeks, we became friends.

Ken was born in San Francisco to a mother who was seventeen. She gave him over to state custody and he was moved from one foster home to another where he was physically, emotionally, and sexually abused. At one home, he was confined to a basement for weeks with little food or water.

Ken wrote his story out on a yellow legal pad. "Kids used to tease me all the time, sayin' stuff like, 'yur parents didn't love yu, that's why they gave yu away,'" he wrote. "The thing about hearing that over and over, yu start believin' yu're worthless and nobody cares for yu."

At fourteen, he left the foster system and hit the streets. He moved around, sleeping wherever he could, sweeping chimneys and working odd jobs, making his way from California to the South.

Ken exuded a simultaneous strength and woundedness that took my breath away. He signed his emails and texts with "Ima Nobody," but also had a wicked sense of humor.

"Yu know why people like me?" he texted one day.

"Why?" I texted back. "Because of your mullet?"

"No, cuz I can't talk back!"

A few months before the Vespers service, Ken was admitted to the hospital. His life-threatening tumor was progressing, and its most recent casualty was Ken's ability to swallow. A clear feeding tube was inserted through Ken's nose, but in a fit of frustration, he ripped off the medical tape and pulled the long clear tube out. The next tube was surgically inserted into his abdomen. He moved from the hospital to an understaffed long-term care facility where his clothes and boots were lost. This had happened to him before. When people are perceived as "less than" and "voiceless," when no one is there to advocate with them, things tend to fall through the cracks—wallets, clothes, discharge plans, and more. When Ken was placed on hospice care, we moved him to the Drake Motel— where the stars stayed. His hospice team included our spiritual mentor Scott, who led the Wednesday night Vespers service at Otter Creek.

For most of his life, Ken had been on his own. But now, in his last months, he was surrounded by love, support, and friends. Brett took him on a road trip to Kentucky. Ingrid and I took him to Starbucks, his all-time favorite place, where he shamelessly funneled coffee directly into his gurgling feeding tube. His hospice nurse set up a hot air balloon ride to fulfill his last wish. Gradually, Ken's texting sign-off evolved from "Ima Nobody" to "Ima Somebody." When people feel like they matter, like they belong, something opens in them. Some of the walls they've been constructing for years to protect themselves begin to fall away. To top it all off, on

Easter Sunday, the story of our friendship was featured on the front page of the local paper—"A Life Resurrected," it read.

When we are undergoing seasons of difficult transitions in our lives—bad news, hardship, loss, illness, dying—it's crucial to have support and to be able to make meaning out of these situations on our own terms. When we don't, we lose pieces of ourselves. When we do, sometimes, miraculously, we discover healing through our wounds. This healing was happening for Ken. I wondered if it would someday happen for me.

When people feel like they matter, like they belong, something opens in them. Some of the walls they've been constructing for years to protect themselves begin to fall away.

"It seems to me it took something like this before I met good people," Ken wrote.

Ken shouldn't have had to wait until he was dying to be surrounded with the care he was deprived of as a child, but that's what happened. I thought back to the way I unraveled after my ankle surgery and then looked at Ken and his strength. After the balloon ride and the news article, Ken's sign-off evolved once more to "Ima Rockstar," and then, finally, to "Ima Badass."

Shortly after the service with Ken, the outreach ministry at Otter Creek began diverting nearly all of their outreach calls to me and our interns at Open Table. I was already slammed, and we were struggling with funding. I reached out to one of the ministers for help and support. "Sorry," he texted, "we're out of resources right now. There isn't anything we can do."

I was beginning to learn where my true spiritual home was, and it wasn't within the walls of a wealthy church that was "out of resources," no matter how thankful I was for the role that community played in our lives or how much I loved the people there. My spiritual home was at our weekly Amos House meetings where we met to pray, to read and wrestle with Scripture, to share silence and Communion, and to support one another. It was on the streets. In the camps. Beneath the underpasses. In the condemned and contested spaces where my friends lived and struggled and died. These were the places where I saw radical trust, hospitality, and generosity. These were the places where I saw people giving away their extra food and the very shoes off their feet and hoodies off their backs. These were the places where I found the living God, the living Christ, and the prophets the church too often shuts out.

Cicada Summer

That May, as Ken's body withered, hundreds of millions of cicadas overtook our region, an insurgence thirteen years in the making. During that time, the brood slept deep underground in wombs of soil, sucking on tree sap and roots. Then suddenly, as a unified collective, amber-colored nymphs flashed awake. No one knows for sure why or how. There is such a thing as mystery.

After digging their way through the earth, the nymphs clamor, climb, and cling to any surface they can—tree bark, door frames, windowsills—and their eerie transformation begins. Their soft bodies form brittle, copper, cocoonlike exoskeletons. Within hours, they wriggle free and hang from larval cases with new skin—forest green shells, bulging red eyes, and sketch-work wings. Their empty nitrogen-rich shells cling to everything and litter the ground, nourishing the trees that will, in turn, nourish the next thirteen-year brood.

For weeks, cicada armies buzz overhead, thickening the air like plagues of old. The noise is deafening, inescapable—a clicking, calling, trilling drone. They slam into you as you walk. You go to great lengths to dodge them, swatting them in the air and skipping around them so as not to crunch them underfoot. Their primal purpose is to ensure the next brood's survival. They mate. Carve slits into branches. Lay eggs in limbs, five hundred at a time. The new nymphs hatch, drop to the ground, dig in, and wait patiently for their time to come.

Ken saw the cicadas. He watched as they lived their short and furious lives. And in late August, surrounded by what Ingrid called "framily"—friends-become-family—Ken gave up the ghost and his spirit shed its mortal skin.

"Was he your father?" the lady at the cemetery asked as I filled out the paperwork for his donated plot. I shook my head. "Uncle?" No again. "Brother?"

I told her I was an outreach worker and met Ken on the streets. "He was my friend."

"But don't you get attached?" she asked, squinting.

"That's the point," I said.

We "get attached" because that's what humans do. We form relationships of respect, mutuality, and trust. We have an impact on others, and they have an impact on us. The second we write someone off as only a client, consumer, or case to be managed, we lose a little bit of our humanity too. We all have something to learn from one another.

Ken was buried in a tie-dyed gown as the free-spirited hippie he was at heart. The week before he passed, we had a service for him so he could hear how he had touched our lives. And then, we kept watch with him. We wiped his feverish brow with a cool rag. We rubbed lotion on his ashen feet and hands. Caring for Ken was a responsibility we shared as a community.

When Ken died, he died a Somebody—a Badass—who made his mark and knew he belonged. And that fall, in the absence of Ken and the cicadas, came a new emergence that would wholly sweep me up and both destroy and renew my faith in humanity.

Occupy

Major social movements don't materialize out of thin air. They, like cicadas, have an incubation period. People are pushed underground by repression, and over time, those who survive remember. They wait for the right season to rise up.

It was mid-September of 2011 when hundreds of thousands living in the United States lifted their heads from the dirt and clamored together in the global outcry against corruption, greed, and income inequality. "The American Autumn is here," declared reporters and activists alike, building on the momentum of the Arab Spring and worldwide protests. People were still outraged about the role that bankers, speculators, and Wall Street tycoons had played in the housing crash and recession. Home ownership was on the decline and income inequality was on the rise. After the near crash of the global economy, there was a gaping chasm between what people were calling "the 1 percent"—the hyperelite who owned nearly 40 percent of the wealth in the United States—and "the 99 percent."[1] When the call came for New Yorkers to take over Wall Street—the financial epicenter of the U.S. economy—they did.

In postrecession America, banks and corporations received more protection from lawmakers and elected officials than families whose homes were foreclosed, students who were drowning in debt, and working Americans who saw their savings and retirement accounts gutted. The U.S. Supreme Court's "Citizens United" landmark ruling in 2010 determined that the same First Amendment rights that applied to people would also apply to corporations. The significance of this decision cannot be understated. For the first time in history, a corporation could pour unlimited amounts of cash into local, state, and federal elections. Their money was protected as free speech. This ruling threatened the fabric of our democracy—a system said to be of, by, and for the people. Occupy Wall Street began with the physical occupation of New York's Zuccotti Park on September 17, 2011. Within a few weeks, over fifteen hundred cities had joined in.

Some community organizers hold that there are two forms of power for social and political change: the first is organized money, and the second is organized people. When we don't have money, we organize ourselves. We petition and fight for change. We make noise. We take up strategies and tactics that we hope bring change. We pray with our presence and our feet.

Andrew and I followed the groundswell across the country, glued once again to livestream footage. Tents went up. American flags were printed with white corporate logos replacing the fifty stars. Tensions heightened between protesters and police, who were tasked not with fighting for our democracy but with protecting property and maintaining law and order. Andrew and I watched as hundreds of marchers trying to cross the Brooklyn Bridge were kettled by the NYPD. The police blocked off the exits and made their way into the crowds. Protesters linked arms and police wrenched them apart. Officers trapped others in bright orange nets and pepper-sprayed noncombative women. "The whole world is watching!" the protesters chanted, resurrecting a Vietnam War–era chant. As they cried out, police bent their arms back and fastened their wrists together with zip ties. Over seven hundred people were arrested. The sparks had ignited here.

A couple days later, news spread about an upcoming rally in Nashville in support of Occupy Wall Street. By this point, Andrew and I were students of social movements. We had studied the campaigns, strategies, and tactics of abolitionists, suffragists, freedom riders, sit-in demonstrators, labor organizers, environmental activists, the Wobblies, the Zapatistas, and more. I was enamored with public figures like Ella Baker, Diane Nash, Myles Horton, and John Brown. I thought of the prophets Isaiah, Jeremiah, and Amos. I thought about Monsanto, Corrections Corporations of America (now CoreCivic), and the private hospital chain that bought my father's hospital. I thought of my friends who faced foreclosures, mounting debt, homelessness.

Just as I knew in college that I had to cut out the chains of paper dolls and had to organize the letter-writing campaign, I knew I had to be at that rally. My faith in a God who is present throughout history, who is on the side of the oppressed, and who is always about the work of transformation, compelled me to act. It is the role of people of faith and conscience to stay awake, to raise critical questions about society, to stand on the side of the oppressed, and to refuse to let injustice have the final say.

It is the role of people of faith and conscience to stay awake, to raise critical questions about society, to stand on the side of the oppressed, and to refuse to let injustice have the final say.

Andrew was supportive but couldn't join me at the rally because of another commitment. My friend Lauren, however, was in. She had just come back from a grueling year of teaching in the Mississippi Delta and had joined our work with Open Table and Amos House.

A couple days after the rally, a teach-in was held that included a facilitated discussion about the possibility of a physical occupation in Nashville. That night Occupy Nashville began, and Lauren, Brett, and I went to keep vigil with others on Legislative Plaza.

The plaza is a nexus of sorts. If you were to stand in the center of the cold granite tiles, the Tennessee State Capitol would tower above you to the north. The lawn of city hall would be barely visible several blocks to the east. The downtown public library—a hub for homeless outreach—would stand a block to the south. And a statue of the scantily-clad god of war and the looming Tennessee Towers—the home of various government offices—would rise above you to the west. Beneath the plaza was a network of meeting rooms where lawmakers held committee meetings and debated bills.

We knew there were laws on the books that banned urban camping and that putting a tent on the plaza meant risking arrest. But in a matter of days, the yawning granite transformed into a bustling encampment. The First Amendment protected "the right of the people peaceably to assemble, and to petition the government for a redress of grievances." But would those rights extend to the physical occupation? Surely if the Supreme Court ruled that the money of corporations constituted free speech, then so did our tents.

What drew me to the plaza was the longing for a more equitable society and a truer form of democracy, but what kept me there were the people. It was Jeremiah, the nineteen-year-old atheist who read Karl Marx's *Capital* in junior high. It was D.J., a divinity school friend who was mentored by the legendary civil rights organizer Reverend James Lawson. It was Salina, a Muslim activist, journalist, and mother of three. It was Jane, the lifelong peace activist. It was Tristan, Kate, and the loose collective of anarchist organizers, facilitators, and gardeners living at the Nashville Greenlands. It was Alesandra, the herbalist and healer who handed out Audre Lorde poems. And it was my friends who were unhoused, like Ray, who joined out of both intrigue and necessity.

After the first tents of the occupiers went up, many friends from the streets began to gravitate toward the occupation. Tent City and other camps had been closed and Metro police officers were encouraging unhoused campers to come to the plaza. The plaza was, after all, conveniently located on state—*not* city—property. Not only did Occupy Nashville provide a physical place to exist, but for those who needed it, it also provided a place to belong.

Unlike movements of the past, Occupy featured no charismatic leader at the helm. It was a "leaderless"—or "leaderful"—movement. The idea was that everyone would bring their gifts and agency and that people from more privileged backgrounds would practice "stepping back" while people from marginalized communities would practice "stepping up." Nightly general assembly meetings were facilitated on the plaza, and decisions were made by a process of consensus building—a complicated task for such a large and diverse group of people. The architects of Occupy Wall Street, however, had spent decades learning from collective decision-making processes used by students in the sit-in movement, the anti-nuclear movement, Quaker groups, anarchist collectives, and others.

At its best, Occupy was awe-inspiring and energizing. Communal kitchen tents and food pantries sprang up, where food was collected, prepared, and distributed. It was the whole Gandhian "Be the change you want to see" idea but in a very public, very gritty way. The air was electric and brimming with city smells and people who rejected deodorant. Was this the revolution we had been waiting for? Lauren and I were on the plaza almost nightly for months, and Andrew joined us when he could. We met regular folks, activists, and organizers, and began to form friendships that would change the lay of the land for movement work in our city.

As time passed, however, complexities emerged. The "step up, step back" idea was great in theory, but in practice, some voices were silenced while others prevailed. Infighting ensued with accusations of this person or that being an infiltrator. And as more people from the unhoused community came to live on the plaza, tensions heightened. I became a mediator between housed and unhoused occupiers, and physical violence occasionally erupted. One night a strong, burly, unhoused man, who was dropped off at the plaza by a Metro police officer, severely beat a younger unhoused man. We couldn't break up the fight, so someone called for help and the very police who dropped him off responded. The younger man was rushed to the hospital while the burly man was briefly held in a police car and then promptly, with no charges pressed, released back to the plaza. It was as if these officers wanted to sow violence and division among us.

Then the governor imposed a curfew on the plaza from ten at night to six in the morning. Anyone who defied the curfew would risk arrest. Other Occupy encampments across the country were facing violent midnight raids where nonviolent protesters were beaten, shot with projectiles, pepper sprayed, tear gassed, and arrested. We didn't know what to expect. Many felt like they couldn't risk arrest because of their immigration status, background, job, or health. But many of us felt called to channel the privileges we had in society into challenging inequitable systems and structures. We received legal counsel from attorneys and strategized about our response to the curfew. We facilitated trainings in nonviolent resistance that included wearing bandanas and scarves in case tear gas was used and teaching people how to protect their heads and vital organs if beaten. That night, I wore Ken's soft, faded lime green bandana around my neck and readied myself for whatever was to come.

Crowds and journalists gathered around the plaza, but the ten o'clock curfew passed without incident. As the evening grew cooler, the crowd thinned, and after midnight, a few dozen of us crawled into the remaining tents. We spooned together for warmth with nervous energy pulsing through us. And sure enough, at three in the morning on October 28, 2011, they came for us.

"They're here! Everybody up!" a voice shouted from the cold.

Within minutes, over one hundred Tennessee Highway Patrol officers had surrounded the camp and formed a perimeter around the plaza. Those of us who were prepared to keep the vigil and risk arrest gathered in the center of the plaza as planned. We linked arms and sat together in formation. An officer with a bullhorn gave us a ten-minute warning to leave. As we waited, we read aloud our First Amendment rights to the officers, and when our ten minutes ran out, the officers waded into our formation, pulled us apart, used the pressure point method of digging their thumbs behind the ears of some protesters, and cuffed us with plastic zip-tie cuffs.

"The whole world is watching!" we chanted.

Later that morning, my mom would wake up in South Carolina to a photo of police arresting me in a national news story. I had given her a heads up the day before, and while she and my dad were worried for me, they were never oppositional or dismissive. They sought to understand—to support.

During the arrests, troopers dragged and carried us to the large police bus that awaited. My zip-tie cuffs were loose enough to squeeze my hands out, but the hands of other occupiers were turning blue from lack of circulation. Before we were loaded into the bus, we were tagged with numbers and our photos were taken for Homeland Security.

History had taught me that this was too often how governments responded to their own nonviolent, democracy-loving citizens. "Who do you serve, who do you protect?" chanted people on the sidelines during the arrests. Were we a threat to public safety and health? Of course not. The real threat was from elected officials and lawmakers who were supposed to protect our rights. Instead, they stripped away our rights behind closed doors while their pockets were padded with money from special interest groups and corporations. Yet so much of that was legal now.

The police bus was like nothing I had ever seen. It was all black, twice as big as a tour bus, and the first several rows of seats were surrounded by locked cages. An officer stood on the bus beneath a surveillance camera and watched us with a stone-cold face as we walked back. Perhaps it was nerves, perhaps it was the memory of how singing calmed protesters in past movements, but as we filed into our seats on the police bus, someone started singing "the wheels on the bus go round and round," and everyone broke into laughter. "The cops on the bus say 'move on back,'" we sang together. And they drove us to the police station.

As it turns out, the night court judge on duty refused to press charges against us, so the State of Tennessee held us for a few more hours and wrote out our citations. We were released and another night of arrests followed. Then, the Nashville chapter of the American Civil Liberties Union filed a lawsuit against the State of Tennessee and a federal judge granted a temporary restraining order that required the police to halt arrests.

Rather than fizzling out, we grew. We held teach-ins and marches. We held a statewide rally where a contingent of protesters briefly took over an abandoned state building, and we held a funeral for the U.S. Constitution and the Bill of Rights. Occupy's critique of the private prison industry and Corrections Corporation of America (now CoreCivic) also ramped up.

Gone Too Far

A couple of weeks after the arrests, I was asked to speak at the Vespers service at Otter Creek, as I had done regularly over the years. But this time, something felt different. Andrew and I were still active at the church, but my public involvement in the demonstrations made things feel tense. My task as a speaker was to prepare a reflection about the gospel text in the lectionary that week, which happened to be the parable of the talents—a teaching from the book of Matthew about a master who leaves town and entrusts his property to three servants. To the first servant, the master gives five talents (or bags of gold), to the second he gives two, and to the third he gives one. While the master is away, the first two servants invest the gold, multiplying the master's profit, but the third hides the gold in the ground. When the master comes back, he praises the servants who increased his wealth but is furious with the servant who simply maintained the amount he left.

"You wicked, lazy servant!" says the master. "You knew that I harvest where I have not sown and gather where I have not scattered seed? Well then, you should have put my money on deposit with the bankers, so that when I returned I would have received it back with interest" (Matt. 25:26–27). The parable ends with the third servant being cast out into the darkness "where there will be weeping and gnashing of teeth" (Matt. 25:30). "For whoever has will be given more, and they will have an abundance," the passage asserts, and "Whoever does not have, even what they have will be taken from them" (Matt. 25:29).

I read the text again and again. This master didn't sound like the God I knew, who cautioned against usury and the accumulation of wealth in the face of poverty. This master also didn't jibe with the Jesus who overturned the tables of the moneychangers a few chapters before. The master in this parable sounded more like the bankers, speculators, and Wall Street executives who crashed the global economy. As I was turning this over in my mind and heart, I heard that our spiritual mentor Scott had given a reflection at a different church earlier that week suggesting that the third servant was the true hero of the parable. After all, he, unlike the first and second servants, refused to participate in systems that reap profit from the labor of others and that exist to help the rich get richer.

On the day I was to give my reflection, I noticed that my name was absent from the list of speakers in the church's afternoon email. Then church leaders asked to see the materials I was planning to use and to read my reflection. They were worried about what I would say, worried that if they allowed me to speak, other members might think they were endorsing Occupy. I sent them my reflection. I even compromised and offered to take out the last two paragraphs about Occupy and save them for a discussion or panel down the road. But despite my compromise, less than two hours before the service began, church leaders determined that I could not speak.

"I prayed about it," one elder told me later, "and this is what God told me to do."

In our world, everything is political—the coffee we drink, the produce we eat, the gasoline and clothes we buy, the news sources we watch and read. Everything comes from somewhere, everything has implications, and everything is biased. It is utterly naive to believe that our interpretations of sacred texts don't also have social, political, and economic implications. Throughout history, these very texts have been used to justify both slavery and emancipation, colonization and revolution, civil compliance and civil disobedience, and nearly every economic and political system under the sun. Indeed, much is at stake.

German liberation theologian Dorothee Soelle, who lived through the horrors of the Holocaust, once said, "Bible texts are best read with a pair of glasses made out of today's newspaper."[2]

Contemporary American theologian Walter Brueggemann built on Soelle's idea, cautioning us not to rely too heavily on the newspaper since it has already been edited by special interest groups. Instead, he argues, we must listen to the unfiltered truth of the streets and hold these voices and experiences up against the sacred texts.[3] In this way, we learn to see not only history but also theology from below.

Perhaps church leaders were right to be fearful of an upside-down interpretation of the parable. But how else are we to interpret our sacred texts when the world is on fire? After all, our sacred texts are not static, one-time revelations intended solely for our personal lives. Their stories are constantly unfolding, evolving, and playing out around us in both the private and public spheres.

While this was not the first time I had been silenced as a female member of the church, it was the most painful. I wasn't some outside speaker—I was a longtime member and had been a leader at that very service. I was even willing to compromise. But that wasn't enough. I had less than an hour to decide what to do, so I weighed my options. Would I stay home and avoid the conflict? Would I attend, push past the wishes of the leaders, and try to speak anyway? In the end, I decided to attend the service. As Andrew and I pulled up to the church, I pressed a strip of duct tape over my lips. We made our way to one of the back pews and my heart hammered in my chest. I had been silenced, but I wouldn't be invisible.

My small action sparked discussions and controversy. I had meetings with church leaders who told me they stood by their decision. The pastor, who later apologized, told me that my interpretation of the parable was "interesting" but clearly not what Jesus intended. One of the elders was supportive, but the others were critical. One justified his decision by saying that I was publicly identified with Occupy and that Occupy's recent protests of private prisons had "gone too far."

Archbishop Dom Helder Camara said, "When I give food to the poor, they call me a saint. When I ask why they are poor, they call me a communist."[4] When I spoke about "serving the poor," church leaders patted me on the back, but when I spoke about *why* so many were entrenched in cycles of poverty, they shut me out. I was reminded of the way many white churches responded to the civil rights movement. "You're going too fast," church leaders told activists and organizers. These churches talked about loving their neighbors on Sunday, but when the conversations turned to actively desegregating schools, lunch counters, buses, and restrooms, the activists had gone too far. In other words, charity-oriented love is safe, but justice-oriented love is dangerous.

Charity-oriented love is safe, but justice-oriented love is dangerous.

That Thanksgiving, Andrew and I participated in a potluck-style feast on tables stretching across the granite tiles of the plaza. As we mourned the loss of our church home—where we were introduced to contemplative spirituality, married, and once belonged—we leaned into Amos House, Open Table, and the congregation of activists and organizers who were becoming our community. When my parents and my younger brother and sister came to visit, we had our family Christmas photo taken on the plaza with the state capitol and a handful of tents in the background. While my family came from a more politically conservative context, my parents taught us to think critically, to ask questions, and to live deeply. Even when they didn't fully understand my actions, their support and unconditional love were humbling.

Not everyone back home in South Carolina felt the same way. When the Christmas cards went out, some of my mom's friends at church told her that the photo from the plaza was "an interesting choice."

"A little political, dontcha think?" one said.

Another friend from church reached out to her with a genuine concern that my activism was motivated by "the socialist agenda." She had been listening to a conservative radio show host who had instructed his listeners to look at their church's website to see if they saw anything about social and economic justice. These words, he said, were "code words" for communism. "If you find them," he cautioned, "run as fast as you can." I wanted to tell her it wasn't the socialists who first radicalized me but a working-class Jew executed by the Roman Empire.

"We are called socialists," said philosopher Slavoj Zizek at Zuc- cotti Park before it was raided, "but here there is always socialism for the rich. They say we don't respect private property, but in the 2008 financial crash-down more hard-earned private property was destroyed than if all of us here were to be destroying it night and day for weeks. They tell you we are dreamers. The true dreamers are those who think things can go on indefinitely the way they are."[5]

That year was a season of both losing and finding. I lost my friend Ken, and Andrew and I lost a church community. But in the void, I found a new sense of belonging. And even through the experience of being silenced, I found my voice.

That winter, Andrew and I were at the prison for a service when one of the men read a passage from Ezekiel. In the passage, the prophet comes upon a valley of dry bones. God asks Ezekiel if the scattered bones can live, and Ezekiel says, "You alone know" (Ezek. 37:3). Then God tells Ezekiel to prophesy to the bones, so he does. A great rattling echoes through the valley, and the bones join together with tendons and flesh. But still, there is no breath in them. Ezekiel prophesies once more, beckoning the four winds to breathe life into the slain, and breath enters them. They stand together, a vast army.

We are a clattering, a clamoring, the dry bones rattling. We are rising, inhaling and exhaling the recycled breath of all who have come before us. In this valley, the dead and dying awaken to life.

The sleeping emerge from their holes in the ground. The oppressed begin to grasp their own collective power. And for a moment, we remember, as Mother Teresa said, that we belong to each other. We remember that we are tasked not with "solving" anything but with showing up at the valley again and again, prophesying to the bones and breath, and getting our hands and feet dirty in the struggles of the world.

8

ACCOMPANIMENT

RAIN FELL ON THE GRANITE tiles and gathered in mirror-like pools reflecting pristine segments of city and sky. But night was rolling in, and with it a piercing wind that whipped across the plaza. Leafless cherry trees quaked. The loose ends of blue tarps beat together in a frenzy. A plastic grocery bag escaped from the kitchen tent at Occupy and shot into the air, rising, rising, rising, and then hurling itself toward the capitol like a thrown rock.

I reached for the metal zipper on my jacket and zipped my exhaustion into its embrace. It had been another long day. School. Work. Occupy. Winter was here, and by mid-December most occupations across the country had been raided or shut down. Ours, however, was holding, though tensions were rising like the plastic bag in the wind. I dug my hands in my pockets, found my keys, and headed toward my car.

"Hey!" said a man I'd never seen before. "Hey!" He was hobbling toward me. "Are you that girl who helps the homeless?"

"I am," I said. "I mean, I do."

"I heard about you," he said. "Listen, I just got outta' jail, and I need a sleeping bag real bad. Can you help me out?"

All the supplies in my car had been given out after the last cold spell. I didn't have anything—including the energy to drive anywhere other than home. "I'm so sorry," I started, and then saw my friend Ray walking up with a cigarette in one hand and the leash for his dog Alky in the other. Ray walked like a man who knew where he was going, even when he didn't. He was scrappy, thin, strong, in his mid-forties. His thinning walnut hair curled beneath his cap and around his ears, and a handlebar mustache framed his smile.

Jeannie and I met Ray early in 2010 when we received a call that the police were planning to close his camp. When we went to see what was going on, we found a landscaped area with rock-lined paths, a communal kitchen, a riverfront beach, and half a dozen residents, including Ray. But Ray didn't trust us then. He had lived through too many empty promises from service providers. Jeannie told the police that if they closed the camp before the residents found housing, they would have to arrest us too.

"That's when I knew y'all were for real," Ray told me later. He said he began to let his guard down when he saw the bags beneath our eyes and heard we were willing to be arrested with them. And that was big. Ray knew abandonment well. He, like Ken, hit the streets at age fourteen. We held the camp for several months. In the end, it wasn't the police who took the camp but the hungry waters of the Cumberland during the 2010 flood. Ray, his dog, and one of his campmates moved into Hobson House with the exiled Tent City residents and stayed for several months. From there, Ray moved to an apartment that was managed by a slumlord, and then he hit the streets again. When he heard about Occupy, he set up camp on the plaza with us.

I gave Ray a hug and bent down to pet Alky.

Ray offered his hand to the stranger. "What's up, brother, I'm Ray," he said.

"Hey, man," he said, "I'm not gonna lie, I really need a blanket or something. I got nothin'."

"I got you," said Ray as he motioned to his tent. We walked over and he unzipped the door and rummaged around. He pulled out a thick, queen-sized quilt, most likely the warmest blanket he had, and bundled it up. Ray passed it to the man without thinking twice, and the man thanked him and walked away.

I knew Ray would be colder without his quilt.

"Ray, thank you," I said. "I'll see if I can find more blankets and bring them out soon."

"I know you will," he said with a smile.

I walked to my car, my heart filled with both guilt and awe. I thought of all the times people patted me on the back for "helping the homeless" or being a "good Christian." But it wasn't me they should be applauding. I was willing to return to my warm home and let a man go cold who came to me seeking help. How easy was it for me to collect donations and give them out? It didn't cost me anything. But it cost Ray something. And Stacey and Bama, who had given their clothes to shelter guests. And Smurf and Teresa, who had provided hospitality from their camp. "For I was hungry and you gave me something to eat," said Christ, "I was thirsty and you gave me something to drink, I was a stranger and you invited me in" (Matt. 25:35).

I had accompanied Ray, Stacey, Bama, Smurf, and Teresa during a time of need. And they had accompanied me—and would for years to come. What is so stunning about sharing the journey with others is that there will come a time when we too need someone to come alongside us. We forget that our liberation is bound up in the liberation of others, and that it is often in the walking, the sharing, the breaking of bread, that we find salvation.

Something about seeing Ray brought me back to myself. The last few months had been filled with one-off actions that were powerful but didn't build to anything tangible. There was something missing from my activism, but I couldn't put my finger on what it was.

At this point, Jeannie had transitioned out of outreach work and had reluctantly become the lead chaplain at Riverbend Maximum

Security Institution, the men's prison in Nashville. I say reluctantly because it's a tricky thing for an anarchist to willingly work for the state. But at the end of the day, she served the men inside, not the systems that caged them. We were still meeting every Sunday for Amos House, and I was still working with Ingrid and Hobson House folks a couple times a week, but I knew I couldn't go back to the kind of outreach work I was doing before the flood. It would chew me up and spit me out. If I was going to do this work for the long haul, I knew I had to figure out what that would look like.

Eviction

As the winter set in, Lauren and I joined about a dozen occupiers and formed a housing rights workgroup. We needed to shift our strategies and tactics and focus on campaigns that could build into something. The first fight we undertook was a sophisticated intervention that focused on Chase Bank's pending foreclosure of the home of Ms. Helen Bailey—a seventy-eight-year-old Nashvillian who had been active in the civil rights movement. Instead of allowing her to refinance her loan after the recession, the bank moved forward with foreclosure, as so many banks did—particularly in Black communities. So we got to know Ms. Bailey and helped her fight back. We used Occupy's platform and our campaign made national news. With so much bad press, Chase Bank caved and Ms. Bailey got to keep her home.

After the successful foreclosure prevention, we were able to connect others facing foreclosure with legal support. We connected with housing rights groups across the country like Occupy Our Homes in Atlanta, Seattle Solidarity Network, and Los Angeles Community Action Network. We were interested in moving in the direction of tenants' rights work and knew this was a huge need in our city. But as we were beginning to help others fight unjust evictions, news came down that a bill was being pushed through the Tennessee State Legislature that would evict Occupy

Nashville from Legislative Plaza for good. The bill would further criminalize camping, sleeping, and cooking without a permit on state property, making it a Class A misdemeanor, with a fine of up to $2,500 and a sentence of up to eleven months and twenty-nine days in jail.[1]

We channeled our energy into fighting the bill. We organized, wrote letters, held press conferences, met with elected officials. Some of us brought up the idea of Occupy's strategic withdrawal from the plaza, but too many people were against it, including some occupiers who were unhoused. We tried to convince state legislators that our occupation was an expression of First Amendment rights. "For those of us who occupy," I wrote in a public piece, "our presence is our protest. . . . Our sleep, our bodily presence in public space, is our speech. If the money of corporations constitutes free speech in our nation, so does sleeping, so does camping, so do activities that sustain daily life during times of protest and petition. When organizing money is a protected right but organizing people—whether sleeping or awake, loud or mute, housed or unhoused—is not, something is gravely wrong."

When organizing money is a protected right but organizing people— whether sleeping or awake, loud or mute, housed or unhoused—is not, something is gravely wrong.

Despite our efforts, the legislators had made up their minds and passed the bill. We were being evicted. In the end, one person— an unhoused twenty-four-year-old occupier—was left standing, willing to face jail time to challenge the new law. And ten days after the bill was signed into law, a Tennessee Highway Patrol officer dragged him from his solitary tent and loaded his camping gear into a truck. The last occupier held his arms out to the officers for arrest, but they declined. They knew that if he wasn't cited or arrested, he couldn't challenge the law in court.[2]

A couple weeks later, our housing rights group joined with Amos House to host the Rally for the Right to Exist on the plaza on Palm Sunday. For the rally, a contingent of Vanderbilt students filled a tent with helium balloons and marched it from campus to the plaza. It floated high above our heads, not *on* state property but floating just over it—a not-so-subtle middle finger to lawmakers who voted "yes." All in all, over 150 people came out for the rally, and dozens of us slept out under the open sky, willing to challenge the new law. But again, no arrests were made. This law would not be enforced on predominantly white college and graduate students with reporters watching, but in the dead of night, beneath interstate underpasses and other pieces of state property.

Troublemakers

Fueled by anger and hope, our housing rights group continued to meet. One day, Ray came to the meeting and told us about an apartment complex north of town. He had moved there from Hobson House, hoping to escape homelessness, but found out that living there was just like being on the streets but with four walls around you and less money in your pockets from the rent. Ray took a few of us to the apartment complex to show us the conditions in which hundreds were living. We met single mothers who welcomed us into their homes and showed us the bedbug bites on their toddlers. Roaches scuttled across the walls and floors of every room we entered. We met a man whose bathroom and bedroom were covered in perpetual black mold, whose ceiling had partially caved in, and whose smoke detector wires dangled down from the ceiling like snakes.

We met a wife and mother named Barbara with a host of chronic health issues, whose right leg had been amputated just below the knee. She coughed constantly, partly due to the black mold that bloomed beneath her ancient, dripping AC unit. Barbara was confined to a wheelchair but had no ramp, despite repeated requests to the landlord to move to a more accessible unit. Her husband, Mike, and their adult son adored her and were doing everything they could to get her to her appointments. But Barbara was too heavy to carry, so every time she had to leave the apartment, her husband and son had to help her climb out of her chair to the ground. She would then drag her body over the sharp ledge in front of the door, across the concrete landing, and down the concrete stairs to the parking lot where the men would hoist her back into her chair. She had open wounds on her knees and legs from this dehumanizing routine.

Less than a year later, Barbara would be dead. I received the call on a Saturday morning and arrived just in time to hold her sobbing husband as the paramedics struggled to heave the stretcher with her corpse from her apartment to the ambulance. Barbara's funeral, a small graveside service with a handful of people, was the first I was ever asked to officiate. I did everything I could to honor her life and show her the respect that was lacking at the funeral for the other Barbara so many years before.

Most tenants at the complex didn't have a copy of their lease. There were blown fuse boxes, electric cords twisting through windows, broken fridges, sparking stoves, sewage leaking from upper units, front doors with no deadbolts, faulty locks, and holes in the walls that some tenants stuffed with toilet paper.

"It's nothing more than an advanced tent city," said one resident. But I had seen more dignified dwellings in the woods. The only half-decent units were the apartments that Section 8 residents lived in because of the annual inspections. Everyone else was in a living hell.

After talking with residents, we realized the first step was to host a "Know Your Rights" training session. We partnered with Legal Aid, found an offsite location to host, and had over a dozen tenants show up. But many more opted not to come. The landlord, a small but terrifying woman we'll call "Ms. Chang," had owned the property for over a decade. She had watchdogs—tenants who kept an eye out for "troublemakers"—who reported back to her whatever they saw and then received favorable treatment from her in exchange, including having their repairs fixed in a timely manner. Rumor had it that at least one watchdog was at the training, and the tenants who came feared retaliation. Despite the threat, a core group of leaders emerged and asked for help putting into practice what the attorneys had suggested: documenting damages, finding or requesting their leases, and making written, dated repair requests while keeping copies for themselves.

Just days later, I got a call from Mike. Ms. Chang had gotten the names of all the tenants who attended the training and had been going door to door, threatening people with eviction. "She's trying to intimidate us," he said.

Later that week, Lauren, Ray, our friend Molly from the housing group, and I lugged a printer with us to the apartment complex to help people copy repair requests and their leases. As we were going to the first apartment on our list, one of the tenants from the training called. "Ms. Chang's onto you," she said.

Just then, we heard tires screech and a door slam outside. "She's here!" shouted Ray. We were too far from our car and couldn't risk being found in someone's unit, so we huddled in an empty, open apartment to try to figure out our next move. Ray took the printer and somehow made his way out the front while Ms. Chang was checking the unit next door. But when she came out, we were trapped. And we were trespassing.

We had to think fast. There was nowhere to hide. It was only a matter of time until she found us, and we couldn't risk being caught inside one of her apartments. We ran to the back of the apartment and realized there was a window. The window opened with some coaxing, but the drop was ten feet down. Without other viable options, we hoisted ourselves out of the window one by one, clung to the ledge with our hands, and then lowered ourselves out the window until we dropped. First me, then Lauren, then Molly. Both Lauren and I had cuts on our arms from the window ledge. We were behind the complex and started making our way around to our car when a shrill voice called out from behind us. It was Ms. Chang.

"What are you doing here?" Ms. Chang demanded.

"We're just outreach workers," I said, my heart drumming against my chest.

"We're here to help people," added Lauren, pulling out a resource guide for proof.

Just then, Ray came around the back corner of the building carrying the printer. Ms. Chang recognized him as a former tenant and tore into him. He was nothing more than a troublemaker. She would ban him from the property for life. He needed to get out *now*.

Then she turned to us as her thinning, grayish-white hair lifted in the breeze. She told us that we were nice girls and shouldn't associate ourselves with folks like Ray. I had to bite my tongue. She moved her hands dramatically while she spoke, and her eyes began to fill with crocodile tears. Why did everyone hate her? All the tenants ever did was try to take advantage of her. If the tenants needed anything, they could just come to her. They didn't need us "church people" to come by.

This didn't seem like the right time to bring up how she had denied Barbara an accessible apartment, didn't pay her workers minimum wage, and refused to make the most basic repairs.

We stayed quiet, befuddled by her dramatic display, trying to avoid her retaliation. We left as soon as we could get out of the conversation.

About a week later, Lauren and I went back to take resources to people and to help them document their living conditions. We weren't there long before two police officers showed up.

"Ma'am," one officer said, "we've received a call from the property owner, and we're gonna have to escort you off this property."

"Are you serious?" Lauren asked.

"Yes, ma'am." He showed us the trespass waiver. Our names had been added to Ms. Chang's list of people who were banned from the property.

I couldn't believe it. Ms. Chang got away with treating her tenants worse than animals, and we were the ones being escorted away by the police? And then I remembered. Policing in the United States has always been set up to protect private property over people. And in Tennessee our laws grossly favored the rights of landlords over tenants.

We continued working with the residents remotely. We helped several relocate, and other members of our housing rights group continued visiting. But in the end, most of the tenants were too scared to organize on a larger scale. If we had pushed to have the apartment complex condemned, it would have taken nearly one hundred units of affordable housing off the market.

So what came out of our work on this? We filed multiple code violations, a handful of tenants moved to better apartments, and Barbara got her wheelchair ramp before she died, not from Ms. Chang but from a church that someone in our group had contacted. She lived her last months with a little more dignity than she had before. The most important things that happened, however, were the relationships that formed and the groundwork that was laid—both in our group and in the hearts of the tenants who knew their rights, knew they deserved better, and knew they weren't alone. We were building a kind of solidarity that would come into play years later when a new tenants' rights group emerged, started tenants' unions at local apartment complexes, and won multiple campaigns.

> *"As long as Christ lives and is remembered, his friends will be with those who suffer."*
> —Dorothee Soelle

"As long as Christ lives and is remembered," wrote theologian Dorothee Soelle, "his friends will be with those who suffer. Where no help is possible he appears not as the superior helper but only as the one who walks with those beyond help."[3]

Sometimes we win; sometimes we don't. Sometimes we get to see the end results; sometimes we don't. But when people are living in hell, we descend into hell to accompany them. We bring what buckets of water we have, try to extinguish what flames we can, and pray that others will join us and that maybe, just maybe, the rain will come or we'll get our hands on a hose.

"Live the Questions"

Just as there are different seasons in nature and in the Christian tradition, there are seasons in movement work. There's a time for mobilizing and a time for staying still. There's a time for pushing forward and a time for pulling back.

The summer following Occupy's eviction and our tenants' rights work was, for many of us, a time to slow down, reflect, and heal. As the days grew longer and hotter, the Christian season of Ordinary Time unfurled. I planted my first garden in the tiny plots outside our rented home: basil, mint, lavender, rosemary, green beans, tomatoes, bell peppers. Digging in the dirt grounded me and reminded me of my grandmother's garden. The fragrant smells from drying bundles of herbs in our kitchen resurrected my spirit. And without the nightly meetings, Andrew and I had more time to go on dates—something we desperately needed. We went on walks together, ate at our favorite Mediterranean restaurant, and wandered around art galleries. In our relationship, we provided balance for each other. He was the calm to my chaos; I was the risk to his caution. He drew me inward; I drew him outward. It was a sweet season when I could finally catch my breath.

Later that summer, I was invited to a fully funded retreat in Vermont with other organizers and activists from Philadelphia, Chicago, New York, Puerto Rica, Bolivia, and Argentina. They were radical thinkers, journalists, artists, anarchists, and architects of the Occupy Wall Street and Strike Debt movements. Despite my feelings of inadequacy among these titans, I was embraced by everyone. Throughout the week, we met with movement elders who asked us questions and sat with us as we asked our own.

What was this present moment in history calling us to do, to think, to be?

What about Occupy worked, and how can we replicate that?

What didn't work, and how can we learn from that?

What can we learn from other movements and groups like the Zapatistas from Chiapas who sought to change the world without taking state power?

These questions lived in me, burned in me, sparked questions of my own life—vocational questions. My head and heart had been so cluttered that I had buried the voices within me that reminded me who I was and helped me listen for where I was being called. I knew I had to quiet the noise around me in order to hear. So I slowed down. I listened.

"Live the questions now," wrote poet Rainer Maria Rilke.[4] And the greatest question I was living was not one of strategy but of vocation. I wanted to keep doing outreach, activism, and organizing, but how could that be sustainable? Most people I knew doing that work burned out or were wildly unhealthy. There was something deeply sacred about accompanying people who were living in the shadows and working with people who were on the frontlines fighting for change, but in the secular nonprofit and movement spaces I had experienced, there wasn't a lot of time or room to explore that sacredness.

On the other hand, at divinity school I felt like something was missing too. I was drawn to pastoral care classes that explored the sacred work of providing emotional and spiritual care in an interfaith context. This work involved cultivating a greater sense of healing and wholeness in myself and others. The problem, however, was that I saw pastoral care being offered only through institutions—hospitals, jails, churches, and other facilities. But my people were on the streets—huddled under bridges and marching with protest signs—and there was a deep-seated distrust of institutions and authority figures. How would my friends ever be able to access those healing resources? I knew that my vocational interests dwelled in the places where the sacred and spiritual collided with the practical—with the everyday life of people who are marginalized and oppressed in our society. But what did that look like on the ground?

The year before, my former boss at Park Center told me about a United Church of Christ minister in Seattle named Craig Rennebohm. Rennebohm had been a street chaplain since the 1980s, and while I had never heard of a "street chaplain" before, I was intrigued.

As it turns out, Rennebohm was a close friend of Ken Kraybill and worked alongside him to pioneer the relational outreach model in which we were trained at Park Center. He founded a nonprofit called the Mental Health Chaplaincy, and his ministry was one of accompaniment. The word "accompaniment," I would learn, was taken from the word "companion," which literally means "one who breaks bread with another" (*com* being Latin for "together with," and *panis* being Latin for "bread"). In Seattle, Rennebohm worked closely with people on the streets and with congregations. He offered outreach support and training to the churches so they could better understand mental health issues and better "companion" people on the margins. In turn, the congregations supported his work financially.

How has he done this work for nearly thirty years? I wondered. I knew I needed to meet him and learn from him. Vanderbilt Divinity School offered Imagination Grants to students, so I wrote a proposal to shadow Rennebohm during the summer, and it was approved. Andrew came with me to Seattle, and after my time with Rennebohm and his colleagues, we had a long-overdue vacation together. But something was still missing. While I loved my time with such kindred spirits in Seattle, they spoke less directly to issues of injustice and systemic change. For that, I would need to learn from someone else. That someone else was Archbishop Oscar Romero.

Andrew and I were both introduced to Romero's life and work in college. Our beloved Biblical Ethics professor, Dr. Lee Camp, showed our class *Romero*, a film about his life that left us rattled. Never had I seen a government so brutal and a minister so willing to take a public stance against oppression. But Romero hadn't always been so radical. Before he was appointed archbishop of one of the largest cities in Central America, he was the kind of guy that people in power considered safe. He was socially conservative and didn't make a lot of noise. And in a country like El Salvador, which was on the brink of civil war, people in power wanted someone they could control. Romero was installed as archbishop in 1977, but shortly thereafter he was jolted by the assassination of his close friend, a fellow priest who had been working with campesinos in a poor village nearby. "The true reason for his death," said Romero, referring to his friend, "was his prophetic and pastoral efforts to raise the consciousness of the people throughout his parish. . . . He was making them aware of their dignity as individuals, of their basic rights."[5]

Romero began to pay closer attention to the struggles of the poor and to listen to campesinos. They told him horrific stories about how their sons, daughters, and relatives were "disappeared" by government-sponsored death squads. It seemed that anyone who spoke out about land reform, economic inequality, and a growing concentration of wealth and political corruption was kidnapped, silenced, tortured, or killed. This was, of course, the age of Cold War anti-communism, and El Salvador's government found a powerful ally in the United States, which backed them financially, trained their death squads, and offered tactical support to the military.

The more Romero accompanied the campesinos, the more he realized that he couldn't be complicit in their suffering. While some people in power criticized him for meddling in politics, he simply replied that he was defending the image of God in human beings. Romero took a stand on the side of the poor that put him in direct opposition to the powers that be, and on March 24, 1980, he was assassinated while serving Mass. Make no mistake—Romero knew what his stance might cost him. He knew there was nothing safe about the gospel. And he knew that it was only through incarnated actions and "authentic solidarity with the poor"[6] that the church would fulfill its true purpose of being "a sign and sacrament of salvation."[7]

Through his ministry, Romero, like his assassinated friend, blended the pastoral and prophetic in ways that moved me. Studying Romero and Rennebohm made me wonder what it could look like to combine the practical aspects of homeless outreach, the pastoral aspects of chaplaincy, and the prophetic aspects of organizing and activism. The idea of street chaplaincy kept coming back to me, so I dug into chaplaincy's historical roots to see what I could find.

As it turns out, chaplaincy's roots date back to the fourth century, just after Constantine converted to Christianity and paved the way for it to become the official state religion of the Roman Empire. One night, a soldier named Martin was returning on horseback to his military base in France. As he was approaching the city gates, he came across a poor beggar who was freezing. Moved by compassion, Martin cut his military cloak in two. He wrapped one half around the freezing man, kept the other for himself, and returned to the base. That night, as he slept, he saw a vision of Christ wrapped in the cloak. "Here is Martin," said Jesus in the dream, "a soldier who is not even baptized, and he has clad me." This profoundly impacted Martin, and he told everyone about it. He was later baptized into the Catholic church and left the military as a conscientious objector. Martin poured himself into studies, became a monk, and then, reluctantly, became the bishop of Tours, France.

As time passed and the legend of St. Martin grew, the remaining half of his cloak became a holy relic and was taken into battle as a symbol of God's presence and favor. This little cloak, or *cappa* in Latin, was kept in a *capella*, or chapel, and the guardian who traveled with the cloak was called a *capellanu*, or chaplain.[8]

For most of recorded history, however, instead of serving and accompanying the poor, chaplains served the royal, wealthy, and elite. In the centuries following St. Martin's death, chaplains served in the palace, looked after sacred relics, and performed Mass for the king. They were also appointed to serve monarchs, nobles, and other members of the aristocracy and, beginning in the eighth century, the military.

To take chaplaincy back to its roots, then, meant taking the tradition back outside the gates of power and bearing witness to Jesus's radical identification with the poor and to St. Martin's act of mercy and solidarity on the streets. This kind of chaplaincy— street chaplaincy—called to me. It made sense when nothing else did. It helped me to better understand my role in all the suffering and oppression around me. Occupy had taught me that injustice must be countered with radical and embodied acts of solidarity. Ray taught me that I didn't have to do this work alone. My work with the housing rights group taught me the importance of proximity and relationships. Rennebohm and Romero taught me to blend the pastoral with the prophetic.

Gradually, I was learning that I wasn't called to fix or save. I wasn't called to single-handedly right the wrongs of the world. I was called to the work of presence and accompaniment. And despite the hardships that would come from such a calling, I knew that I would find my own salvation through the walking, the sharing, the breaking of bread.

9

WICK

IF YOU COULD HAVE BEEN THERE the night Jimmy Fulmer died, it would have sounded like this: Jimmy's crutches clicking on sidewalk. The occasional swoosh of cars passing him by. Dogs yapping from fenced-in yards. Bare branches of hackberries and oaks scraping together in protest against the piercing January wind.

Jimmy couldn't make it far. He had no bus fare and no place to lay his head. He managed to crutch to an empty church in East Nashville—locked, as many churches are on such nights. He curled up on the cold stone steps alone.

The only person who stopped to check on Jimmy was his friend Wilford Gold, who also lived on the streets. Wilford saw that Jimmy didn't have a blanket. Like a modern-day St. Martin with no money in his pockets and no military cloak to split, he panhandled enough to buy a sky-blue blanket from a nearby dollar store and took it back to Jimmy.

But here's the thing. The human body isn't designed to survive in extreme cold, even with the benefit of a blanket. First, it shivers uncontrollably, trying to produce more warmth. Next, blood flow migrates from the extremities to the core. Hands and feet burn as if on fire. Then, a numbness sets in and the body goes on autopilot. The primary command: protect vital organs. Toes, fingers, and feet? They can go. Later, an enormous fatigue sets in. For some, a primal instinct takes over and they try to burrow into small, covered spaces. For others, any movement feels impossible, like their bodies have become hunks of lead. Before the organs give out, breathing becomes so shallow that loss of consciousness ensues, which is, perhaps, a small grace. The dying don't fade, however, before knowing the loneliness, sting, and terror of the biting cold.

I was haunted by Jimmy's death. What were his last thoughts? Did he feel confusion, comfort, despair? Did he see pieces of his life flash before his eyes? Was the utter darkness that surrounded him sudden, or was it gradual like the measured turning off of lights?

Wilford came back to check on Jimmy early the next morning and found his breathless body beneath the blanket, his crutches propped against the church's cold stone steps. He called 911 from a nearby gas station.

Cold Anger

The public death of Jimmy Fulmer lit something in me and others across the city. All winter, Open Table Nashville—our scrappy nonprofit with only a couple paid staff members and a small army of volunteers—had been opening emergency shelters for people who couldn't or wouldn't go to traditional shelters. But we couldn't do it alone. We had tapped every faith community we could, as had other nonprofits. Where was the Office of Emergency Management? Where was the Red Cross? When the private sector can't or won't meet the needs, the public sector, as stewards of the common good, must step up.

The week after Jimmy died, our housing rights group organized a funeral procession to draw attention to the need for more emergency shelters and housing.[1] Those in movement communities understand that mobilization and systemic change are sometimes

144

possible only after a crisis. Without something startling, there's not enough fuel to wake people up and unite them. We knew that the outrage we felt had to be channeled into action, so we marched a heavy wooden coffin from the park in front of the downtown library to the Homelessness Commission's monthly meeting over a mile away.

"No more death on the streets!" we chanted.

"What do we want?" someone shouted.

"Housing!" we answered.

"When do we want it?"

"Now!"

A new power was building from below. Of the people who marched, many were currently or formerly unhoused, some were friends of Jimmy, some were former Power Project members. There were students, activists, clergy, service providers, and even sympathetic city commissioners. Our feet prayed for change as our voices united in the frigid morning air.

I first read about the idea of channeling collective anger in Mary Beth Rogers's book *Cold Anger*.[2] Hot anger, Rogers says, is the kind of anger that seizes you up. It is wild and burns everything in its wake. Hot anger destroys, and sometimes our structures and systems need to be leveled, burned to the ground. But other times, we need to cool our anger so it can be channeled and directed.

Hot anger destroys, and sometimes our structures and systems need to be leveled, burned to the ground. But other times, we need to cool our anger so it can be channeled and directed.

Somehow, Jimmy's death felt like it encompassed all the deaths of our brothers, sisters, and siblings on the streets, so after we mourned and beat the pavement with our tears, our fury, our feet, we channeled our collective anger into a demand that would be realized in just over a year's time: that the city take part in providing emergency shelter for those with barriers to traditional shelters. Jimmy and all the others we lost on the streets would not die in vain.

That spring, as the cherry trees, dogwoods, and redbuds blazed, I filled my time with meetings, writing papers, and trying to figure out what to do with my life after graduate school. I was graduating with a master of theological studies degree and knew I wanted to find a way to do the outreach, organizing, and maybe even street chaplaincy. Andrew was also in the midst of discerning his calling. Would he keep editing *The Contributor* or would he apply for doctoral programs? I wanted to work on the streets with Open Table Nashville, but we were barely scraping by. If I was going to work there, I'd have to raise my own salary. And if I was going to raise my own salary, I needed to begin drawing up a proposal to present to possible funders. That spring and summer, however, I couldn't focus on paperwork. There were meetings, protests, actions, and marches every week. Activists and organizers from across issues—workers' rights, food justice, immigrant rights, housing rights—were coming together in solidarity, showing up for each other in new ways. The collective power that was building in our city was, in part, the child of Occupy and all the relationships that had been formed or strengthened on the plaza. The noise around me was inspiring, but it was also deafening.

My pro-bono outreach work and side hustles hadn't let up either. What I desperately needed to balance it all was clarity, and that clarity wouldn't be found in the chaos. So I set off to the Abbey of Gethsemani in Kentucky, where Thomas Merton had lived as a monk. "The whole world is secretly on fire," Merton wrote, reflecting on how difficult it is to be still when even the silence around us is ablaze.[3]

"Be Ignited"

Drive 140 miles north of Nashville, meander slightly east of New Haven, and there stands a Trappist monastery built in 1851, nestled between the slow rolling hills and farmland of Kentucky. No matter how much I loved Nashville, leaving it felt like detox. On the drive, the concrete and bustle of the city fell away, filling the asphalt horizon with the rock walls and the emerald green of trees that rose around me. Perhaps it was the surroundings, perhaps it was the distance, but the anxiety in my chest began to loosen and my breathing deepened for the first time in a long time. When I got off the interstate, I rolled down the windows and warm July air rushed around me, tangling my hair. I drove alongside rows of tobacco and corn, old silos and barns, fields of livestock—a slower, seemingly simpler way of life. I smiled with every mile as a giddy anticipation rooted itself in me.

Andrew had been on solo retreats at Gethsemani before, so I knew a little about what to expect. Why had I waited so long before coming? He had encouraged me to come years before and knew I needed this. But I was still too good at putting my own health on the back burner.

The abbey had a retreat center that was attached to a main sanctuary. The sanctuary was attached to the monks' quarters. The abbey's architecture was marked with a calming simplicity: white exterior walls, rectangular and triangular windows, a rust red roof on the monks' side, and a sea green roof on the retreat side. The retreat center was a place of silence with just a few places designated for speaking. The silence folded itself around me like a long-lost friend. I turned off my phone and locked it in my car, content to tell the time by the ringing of the abbey bells and the alarm clock in my room. I was staying on the third floor, and my window looked over a small private garden for the monks that held a koi pond and a magnificent gingko tree. Inscribed over the gate to the garden were the words of the psalmist: "God Alone."

Seven times a day, the monks hold services in the main sanctuary to "keep the hours." Vigils, Lauds, Terce, Sext, None, Vespers, and Compline. I went several times a day, the chants and prayers filtering through my inner chaos, cleansing me, reminding me who

I was. The monks prayed for the poor and sick. They prayed for peace.

Surely this is why the world hasn't imploded yet, I thought. *It's because monks and nuns are praying like this, keeping the hours, keeping watch.*

Every night, I witnessed the sun sink beneath the blue Kentucky horizon from the top of a small hill just outside the monastery. The colors blushed in a frenzy and then gradually cooled, settling into a sea of indigo night. As the sun set before me, the moon rose behind me, bright and full. I remember hearing somewhere that no matter what the moon looked like to us on earth, it is always whole. I longed for that kind of wholeness.

The second night, I sat at the desk in my room with over ten years of old journals stacked around me. I had come to the abbey not only for silence and rest but also to listen to my life and discern where I was being called. As I looked out over the "God Alone" garden, the moon peered in at me, beckoning me inward.

Just then, I was flooded with memories of a dream I had years before. I found myself inside the dream again, standing in the immense lobby of a church I didn't recognize. The architecture was modern, and the walls were painted a churchy taupe. Morning light filtered through the windows, casting a warm glow around all the Sunday churchgoers. While people were catching up on the latest gossip before the service, I looked over toward the side of the lobby near the front door and gasped. I cupped my hand over my mouth. Did other people not see what I saw? There was a man in his late twenties or early thirties with his right arm chained to the ceiling. Why did no one else seem to care? He looked like he had been there for months or years. His unkempt hair tangled around his shoulders, and there was something ancient about him. He didn't do or say anything to draw attention to himself. He just stood there, looking directly at me with grave, imploring eyes.

Should I ask the church leaders to unlock the chains? A resounding *no* echoed through me. Better to ask forgiveness than permission, I thought. Something in me pushed me toward him: an enormous compassion, sorrow, and disbelief. I climbed up on the counter next to the man and somehow managed to take the chains down. The man said nothing. He just stretched out his arm and nursed his wrist. A few other people in the lobby noticed what I had done but seemed largely indifferent.

My memory of the dream faded, and the warm light of the lobby funneled into the cool darkness of the abbey. I laid there pondering the meaning of the dream for some time. Who was the man? Why did his calm, gripping eyes haunt me still? Was I the person whose hand was chained to the ceiling of the church, or did I help free someone else from such bondage? As the moon smiled in on me through my window at the abbey, the meaning of the dream became clear as the night sky.

I was raised in the Churches of Christ, and from early on in my life, church was where I learned to love God and neighbor. It was where I saw people taking care of each other, where I found meaning and purpose and hope. But church was also where I saw and felt immense exclusion, where I heard that the calling to ministry was extended only to men and that God's love and, ultimately, salvation were extended only to certain kinds of people who followed certain rules and fit in certain boxes.

As I grew older, some of the walls that had been constructed in me to keep certain people out, to keep God in, and to keep the boat from rocking, slowly began to crumble. The physical walls of the church building began to close in around me, and I felt trapped. At the same time, I began to see and experience God more in the margins of society—the tent cities, jails, streets, and public squares—than I did within the actual walls of the church. I joined together with others who felt like refugees from the institutional church and we formed Amos House. This became our church. It developed organically and was unconventional, unpropertied, unbound, physically homeless, experimental, and ecumenical. In these ways, it was like the Spirit of God.

Over the years, we at Amos House had created a space where I could participate in the liturgical rhythms that brought me life, where I was filled and nurtured, where I found rest, and where I could bring my whole self—my doubts and convictions, my questions and hopes. Amos House helped undo the chains that were holding me captive to a life of guilt, unworthiness, mediocrity, and exclusion. Together, we dared to ask why we would ever keep the flames in our bellies and bones that so desperately need to be unleashed on a lukewarm world. "Be ignited, or be gone," wrote the poet Mary Oliver.[4]

I had spent the past couple days at Gethsemani reading back through over ten years of my journals that were now stacked beside me on the moonlit desk. The entries traced my faith that started out focused on personal salvation and later became about both personal and societal transformation. They revealed my journey through the world of literature and ideas, as well as my lived experiences with people who were exploited and unhoused. They bore witness to my anxieties, exhaustion, and sorrows, but they also illuminated moments of peace and presence, of life and wholeness.

As I read back through my experiences in late high school and early college, I saw that the doors that might have been opened to me as a man in the Churches of Christ were closed because I was a woman. I read through entries about planning Sunday night church services that the youth group boys led for our church. Even though I helped orchestrate the services, I couldn't participate in leading them. I read through pages of vocational discernment as I expressed my interest in theology and different forms of ministry. I couldn't, however, figure out how to channel those interests. I didn't want to be a secretary or children's minister, which is what I was told my options were in my denomination. It didn't even dawn on me that I could consider entering into some type of ministry or pastoral role; women in our denomination weren't allowed to do that.

So I silenced the still, small voice—that spark—inside of me for over a decade. Even when I started divinity school three years earlier, I didn't really believe that I, a woman, could preach or do pastoral work. It was only through witnessing the courageous and compelling lives and work of women like Dorothy Day, Jeannie, and others that this belief began to shift. I realized that the notion that only men can be ministers didn't come from God but from people and churches who failed to grasp that God can speak and work through women and all people in the same way that God can speak and work through men. I realized that perhaps I too could rekindle the spark inside me and pursue some form of ministry.

When I took a preaching class during graduate school, my mom asked if I would send her one of my sermons so she could read it. In order to even write or preach a sermon—something I felt completely ill-equipped to do—I had to turn to other women who had found their voices: authors and priests like Barbara Brown Taylor and local nonprofit leader Becca Stevens. I watched videos of them preaching and read their books. After I managed to write my first sermon, I sent it to my mom, and she shared it with my dad. When I asked my dad about it over a break, he couldn't bring himself to call it a sermon.

"Your paper was . . . interesting," he said, pausing with uncertainty.

My dad and I, united by our calling to heal and our deep sense of spirituality, disagreed often about theology, white privilege, LGBTQIA+ issues, and a woman's place in the church. But there were bits of openness in him. And there was love. He was an elder at my former church, a conservative Church of Christ congregation, and was gradually helping to broaden their perspective on what he called the nonessential elements of salvation that so many believed were crucial "to get into heaven"—like the absence of instruments in worship. Later, my dad would tell me that he didn't have a vocabulary for the things I was bringing up in our discussions. And how could he? His world was entirely different from mine.

What would he say if I told him I felt called to chaplaincy, to ordained ministry? And what would my path to ordination even be? The Churches of Christ not only didn't have a formal process for ordination but they also didn't recognize women as ministers. If I were a man; if I could pray, preach, and lead hymns; if I could land a preaching job, then voilà! I was a minister. Now, my church home was Amos House. We were registered as a church and met weekly. We all shared tasks and roles, but Jeannie, who was ordained by a community church in Atlanta whose members were largely unhoused, was on record as the lead minister. Could Amos House ordain me? Would they?

At the end of the day, ordination is the process where a church or denomination recognizes and affirms the calling from God upon one of their members to a particular kind of public ministry. While that calling ultimately comes from the Spirit of God, ordination is the act of a community to appoint and send out someone in their name to preach and embody the gospel.

But I didn't feel called to be a minister to a physical church. I felt myself being called to people on the streets and in the abandoned, undomesticated spaces in our society. I was called to reimagine what ritual and liturgy could look like in the margins of our society, and I wanted to be able to practice street chaplaincy to the fullest—to serve Communion, baptize, and perform marriages and funerals when those sacraments and services were requested. I was called to a ministry without walls, a ministry that valued the spiritual life of contemplation and prayer as much as it valued an active life of struggling alongside those who struggle. This kind of ministry understood that the "kin-dom" of God, the beloved community, was not merely an otherworldly destination for our souls, but a horizon—something that was always beyond us but also beneath our very feet.[5] The only kind of conversion I was interested in was converting the black and red ink of Scripture into living, breathing flesh. I wanted to follow in the footsteps of a homeless Galilean who spent his time on the underside of society, who balanced healing and teaching with raising holy hell.

While I was at Gethsemani, I wrote a letter to members of Amos House about this calling I felt toward ordination. I read it to them when I came back, and we spent the next season in discernment and conversation. Andrew offered unconditional support, believing in me when I struggled to believe in myself. I met one-on-one with members of Amos House and my friends on the streets. When I met with Jeannie and asked her about the possibility of being ordained through Amos House, she leaned in, gleaming like the moon.

I wanted to follow in the footsteps of a homeless Galilean who spent his time on the underside of society, who balanced healing and teaching with raising holy hell.

"Why not?" she said. "You're already living this out. It's who you are. Ordination is just a way to make it legit."

I met with Charlie the next week. He had been a priest in the Catholic church until he gave up his formal title as "Father" to serve his nonprofit instead of a parish. I was worried about what he might say, but he had been a spiritual mentor to me. I valued his insights and opinions. After I told him, he too smiled warmly.

"Here's the way I see it," he said. "We make it all up anyway. All our churches and institutions make up processes and rules, and they're somehow official. But only God calls someone to ministry. Only God ordains."

It was set. We picked a date and place—October 13, 2013, at the old Tent City—and began planning the ordination service. Yet, there were still two more people I needed to talk with: my mom and dad. I wrote them a letter, explaining everything and inviting them to come to and participate in the service. After they got the letter, I called them. My mom picked up.

"Of course we'll be there," she said, ever the supporter. She passed the phone to my dad, and my heart quickened. There was a pause that morphed into a small eternity in my mind.

Then, I heard his voice. "I guess we're coming to Nashville," he said with surprising tenderness. My eyes brimmed with tears. So many parents choose a different response when their children step out of their shadow. In some small way, this felt like a coming-out moment for me. There was something about my identity that fundamentally clashed with what my dad had believed for decades. But instead of arguing with me or rejecting this part of me, he chose to support, love, and affirm all of who I am.

What would people say back at church? As an elder, how would he explain *this*? When a church member accused me of socialism, it was one thing. Being a female minister was something else altogether. It was an affront to the patriarchal traditions that had been upheld for centuries. To this day, I've never asked my dad why he was so willing to support me, but I knew his love for me outweighed any of his concerns. When our call ended, I let out a long sigh of relief and wiped the salty stream of tears from my cheeks. What I didn't realize until that moment was how much his support meant to me and how much I needed his acceptance. Instead of perpetuating the cycle of exclusion, he had broken it.

Lit

Dust rose up around our feet as we walked the familiar footpath. October light filtered through the trees that were just beginning to catch flame with the yellow-ambers of autumn. We found a clearing and spread blankets and quilts out on the ground in the old Tent City. Lauren and my friends from Amos House brought programs, vases full of zinnias, and folding chairs and tables for the service. A host of familiar faces trickled down the path until the clearing was filled with family members and friends—both housed and unhoused—who meant the world to me. I walked over to Andrew, and he wrapped me in a tight hug. "I'm so proud of you," he beamed.

Before the service, my friend Vegas, who had once called this clearing home, discovered that the cherry tomatoes he had planted at the camp before the flood in 2010 had come back. They were flourishing in the forsaken soil. He and Jeannie grabbed a handful and brought them to the service. I wish I could remember all the details from that day. I was so overwhelmed by the love and support I felt. I was so intent on being present in every moment that the words and events washed over me like a kind of baptism.

I remember that when Charlie prayed, I flashed back to the rally at city hall, where he had prayed over me and offered me a kind of anointing for the journey that would lead me here. When it came time for my "charge to ministry," a myriad of voices rose up, exhorting me to keep wrestling with Scripture, embracing seasons of wilderness, welcoming the outcast, honoring rhythms of Sabbath, and working toward collective liberation in the margins. Jeannie served as the officiant for the event, and toward the end she invited me up to the front. While our friends sang "Wade in the Water," she faced me and placed a cross of oil on my forehead. She took both my hands in hers and anointed my palms and then bent down and anointed my bare feet. She hugged me and placed a stole Lauren had made for me over my head. The stole was made of a kind of material that looked like burlap and had dark brown felt symbols stitched onto the front: a dove and flames on one side and a Chi-Rho—a symbol used by early Christians to represent Christ—on the other. Then, Jeannie introduced me to my community as the Reverend Lindsey Krinks. Time slowed and I looked across the crowd. My friends cheered, and I felt utterly surrounded by light. So much of what was said that day I have forgotten. But one thing that Jeannie said will stay with me as long as I draw breath: "You are wick," she said, locking eyes with me. And I knew she was right.

We are not the flame. We are not the fuel. We are wick, ready to be lit by the living God, ready to burn, to bring warmth to those freezing in the shadows, and to light the lukewarm world aflame.

10

TENDING WOUNDS

THE SANCTUARY at Green Street Church of Christ didn't smell like incense; instead, the humble sanctuary of one of the smallest, poorest churches in Nashville smelled like unwashed bodies and cigarette smoke. Outside, the cold hurled against the brick exterior, pushing through any crack it could find. The church leaders, all unpaid, worried about the heat bill, but what was the alternative? To leave people out in the cold? Absolutely not. God would make a way.

Throughout the winter of 2013–14, one of the coldest winters on record, sleeping bags and fraying quilts draped across Green Street's pews. On the raised platform by the altar, an elderly couple curled together in a nest of blankets. At night, hymns of heavy snoring, wheezing, and incessant coughing rose like a petition—or maybe even praise. Despite the coffee, urine, and blood-stained carpet, Green Street's sanctuary was the holiest sanctuary in our city.

Normally when Green Street opened their doors in the cold, it was just for the campers who lived on their tiny plot of land. After Tent City was closed in 2010 and Occupy's camp was evicted in

2012, people who came to their weekly meals began asking for permission to camp on their land. First, it was a fierce, tiny woman named Ms. Linda. After praying about it and discussing it, the church leaders responded, "We're not going to tell you that you can, but we're also not going to tell you that you can't."

"We realized," one of the deacons told me later, "that the church property wasn't *our* property. It was God's. And we were called to use it faithfully for God's people."

After a few more campers set up tents beside Ms. Linda, Green Street received notice that the tents violated Metro's zoning ordinances. Failure to dismantle the camp would result in fines and further legal action. The church leaders decided that ultimately, they didn't answer to Metro; they answered to God. The tents would stay.

Now here's a church I can get behind! I thought. I worked with another homeless advocate, and we connected church leaders with an attorney named Tripp Hunt, who had represented protestors during Occupy. Tripp looked like a monk in a suit—bald, thoughtful, and composed. He had a joint degree in law and divinity and agreed to represent the church for free. He knew religious land-use laws inside and out and knew that, thanks to the Religious Land Use and Institutionalized Persons Act (which we had tried to use in Antioch), the freedom of religion overrode the government's ability to impose certain zoning requirements. Green Street fought the city and won. They also sought to win over nearby businesses by cutting their grass for free and being good neighbors.

In extreme weather, they opened up their building so the twenty or so campers could sleep in the classrooms downstairs. This particular winter, however, the need was even greater. The weather barely crawled above freezing for weeks at a time, and some nights the wind chills dipped below zero.

Open Table Nashville mobilized to open a few churches every night the temperature dropped. The churches we opened were compassionate and maybe even reckless enough to let us bring in whomever we found—the sickest of the sick, the roughest of the rough, the couples and pet owners, and those who were banned from other shelters or too jaded, paranoid, or intoxicated to go in elsewhere. Green Street was one of those churches, and when the classrooms and fellowship hall were full, they opened their sanctuary.

Some nights at the shelters were energizing and inspiring. Shelter guests pitched in, gave up the more comfortable spots for people who were older or sicker, and helped with clean-up. But there were also nights that were exhausting and discouraging. Fights broke out. Grown men directed sexist comments at me and others, made racist remarks, pulled knives on one another, and stole what they could find. We had to remind ourselves that beneath the hatred and anger was trauma, desperation, and the need to grasp for control or prove themselves. While we had rules and kept boundaries, we also tried to work with everyone we could. We were there, after all, not just to tend the wounds of the people who were polite and followed the rules. Jesus said, "It is not the healthy who need a doctor, but the sick" (Luke 5:31).

And yet every sixteen-hour day reminded us that the need was for so much more than shelters. The shelters served as a bandage on a festering system. Ultimately, what we needed was more affordable, accessible housing. What we needed was a shift in power and the creation of an economic system that no longer crushed the poor. Dietrich Bonhoeffer has been credited with saying, "We are not to simply bandage the wounds of victims beneath the wheels of injustice, we are to drive a spoke into the wheel itself."

The work of accompaniment calls us to move from models of service to models of solidarity.

The work of accompaniment calls us to move from models of service to models of solidarity. And while the word "solidarity" is flashy and even alluring, putting it into practice is anything but. Solidarity involves putting your body, your heart, and even some of your relationships on the line. Solidarity means that you carry part of the immense injustice in the world alongside others because no one should bear that weight alone. It means you take risks, give up comforts, share resources, struggle alongside others, and sometimes make mistakes.

That winter, practicing solidarity looked like organizing volunteers and faith communities to open extra shelters when our friends were freezing and there wasn't enough room in the inn. We were exhausted. We got sick—sharing the diseases of our friends. Our backs ached from sleeping on pews and fellowship hall floors. We gave up certain comforts but gained so much more. Some nights, we even caught a flicker of the Beloved Community in our midst.

Pick-a-Tree Village

Canisters of propane weighed down our backpacks as Lauren and I searched for the right footpath along the Greenway just north of town. A man who came to one of her shelters needed supplies, so we had set out with propane, bags of food, and winter gear. The smell of sulfur from a nearby plant carried on each cold gust of wind and stung our noses. As we turned a curve, we found a well-worn path that bowed toward the Cumberland River. Mud squished beneath our boots and amber-gray grass brushed against our jeans. The path dipped through a gully and then let out on higher ground to a clearing with a well-established camp.

"Knock knock, anyone home?" Lauren shouted as we walked. "We're outreach workers, just coming to check on folks."

A wooden cross and American flag stood watch over the entrance of the camp. The site, more compound than camp, was flanked on one side by a drop-off that led to the river and by a hill of woods on the other. A plywood fence protected the main living area with several tents, and toward the back of the camp stood two more tents and a cobalt blue port-o-potty.

"Hey there, anybody home?" I called as a rustling rose from behind the fence.

A familiar voice called out to me from behind the plywood fence, "Lindsey, is that you?" A puff of gray hair tied back with a red bandana emerged from the compound's gate.

"Smurf?" I shouted, stunned. I hadn't seen Papa Smurf since just after the flood—nearly four years before. Rumor had it that he and Teresa split up, and after a stint in jail he moved to a camp called "The Bat Cave" that I was never able to find.

Smurf named his well-organized camp "Pick-a-Tree Village." It was home to four men, one woman, driftwood art, a skillfully built brick stove, and a patchwork of colorful tarps laced together with bungee cords. They took in guests; fed the turtles, ducks, and herons; sometimes fought; and protected a family of sparrows nesting in an old backpack hung on the edge of an easel. A creepy yet comical human-sized stuffed Sylvester cat was propped up in a tree, and Happy Meal–sized smurf figurines were propped here and there for decoration. The port-o-potty in the back had been buried in mud after the flood and was salvaged and reclaimed by the men. "This is for the ladies," Smurf said with a wink, pointing to the toilet. After a grand tour, we caught up, exchanged numbers, and promised to be in touch.

In the weeks that followed, the winter gradually dispersed, lifting like early morning fog on the river. With each warmer day, the tender leaf buds unfurled into a canopy of the freshest green I had ever seen. My coworkers and I had gotten to know the other residents at Smurf's camp, and sometimes, after long days of outreach, we'd find ourselves driving to their camp to sit at the river, feed the ducks, and see what feathers Smurf had collected. We'd pull up a chair, recount the struggles and triumphs of the day, laugh, receive, breathe. When the coolness of night settled in, I imagined the campfire was like a Siren, crackling and calling for us to draw near, to turn our minds away from the defeats and fix our attention on the small everyday wonders that surrounded us.

My eyes traced the night-darkened river and the tiny slice of property on which we were trespassing. The men and women at the camp carried their own wounds, but they weren't victims. They were survivors with free spirits that could not be caged. They were there for a myriad of reasons: crowded shelters, long waiting lists, nearly insurmountable barriers to housing, and the human desire to assert some agency over their lives.

"At least here," said Luke, one of the tattooed residents with a long history of incarceration, "we can keep our stuff safe and our fate is in our own hands. We don't have someone breathing down our necks, barking orders every second."

As I was driving home that night, words Smurf said to me years before came surging back to my mind. "My mom once told me," he said, "that once you hit the bottom of the barrel, you gotta stay there and swirl around for a while 'til you can see what's down there and what you're looking up at. Then," he continued, "you gotta take one step up at a time so you don't slip and the ladder doesn't break."

If anyone knew what the bottom of the barrel looked like, it was Smurf and his campmates. Over the course of their lifetimes, they had been boxed in, beaten, caged, strapped down, and stripped of everything. Some grew up in abject poverty, some fought in condemned and horrific wars, and others had been inescapably branded by past circumstances. Their barriers to housing, sobriety, and wholeness felt insurmountable. Despite the occasional peacefulness of the camp that we experienced, there were frequent arguments and fights. Anxiety and despair ravaged their bodies and minds, and when they were overcome, they turned to the bottle and took their frustrations out on each other.

Perhaps these residents weren't swirling around the bottom of the barrel as Smurf had suggested; perhaps they were at the bottom of a deep and gaping hole. And perhaps that hole was dug by our society over decades—centuries—through systemic divestment in the lives of poor, working class, indigenous, and Black and brown communities. The ugly truth is that the ground in our society has never been level for everyone. Since the time of slavery, there have been racial disparities in land and homeownership. Even after the Emancipation Proclamation of 1863, this inequitable chasm was deepened by measures like the Homestead Act in the 1860s and the New Deal in the 1930s. These pieces of legislation largely excluded Black Americans from land grants and homeownership loans and paved the way for more segregated housing and redlining.[1] More dirt was dug out by the deinstitutionalization of mental health care that began in the 1960s and failed to produce an adequate safety net for people with mental health disorders. Then the War on Drugs beginning in the 1970s and Truth in Sentencing laws beginning in the 1980s sent the U.S. prison population soaring. These policies disproportionately impacted Black, brown, and poor communities and led to federal investment in systems of policing and incarceration instead of social, economic, and rehabilitative supports.[2] The hole plummeted deeper still from the gutting of federal funding for affordable housing that began in the 1980s and the failure of minimum wage to keep up with the rising cost of living.[3]

Once you find yourself in the hole, it's nearly impossible to climb out. Yes, the hole we've dug in our society is deep. As people of faith and conscience, our work is not to simply toss down handouts so a few people have enough, or to lower down a ladder so those who are strong enough can climb out. These responses amount to no more than charity. While such charity may be necessary as temporary stopgap measures, it does nothing to disrupt and transform systemic inequities. The work that is desperately needed—the work to which we are called—is to fill in the hole, because that is justice.

Not a Crime

I got Smurf's call at the beginning of Holy Week. "It's a 911 emergency," he said. Early that morning, two police officers had marched into their camp threatening to issue trespassing citations and shut the camp down if they didn't leave. There had been a fight at the camp the week before, and one of the residents had called the police. The officers were using this call to justify the eviction. I drove straight to the camp to help hold a camp meeting with Tripp, the attorney; my coworker Samuel, who left his teaching job at a private school to work with us; and Steve, a retired businessman who had been visiting Smurf's camp with his church group.

"If you want to fight this," we told the residents, "we'll fight this with you. But you have to organize yourselves." We all agreed on the terms. Keep the camp clean. Keep things cool. Handle any arguments internally or call us to mediate. Avoid calling the police whenever possible. If the police come, call us immediately. Get the officers' names, ask for a written notice, and refer them to Tripp who, saint of saints, had agreed to represent them for free.

Lauren made an enormous banner that read "Homelessness Is Not a Crime" and hung it at the camp's entrance. Samuel documented all the residents' belongings in case of a police raid. Ingrid began negotiations with the police. We started to organize volunteers for twenty-four-hour copwatch vigils and used our media contacts to broaden awareness and garner public support.

Ingrid talked with the central precinct commander and explained the situation. We were working with the residents to obtain housing, but they had barriers and the waiting lists were long. It wasn't until the media attention put public pressure on city officials that the police agreed to a thirty-day extension. But a month wasn't enough. We told them the camp needed to stay open until all the residents could obtain housing.

After a couple weeks of police threats, vigils, and more media pressure, we got the good news. The central precinct commander was giving the camp a temporary reprieve: the camp could, barring any unforeseen disaster, remain open until housing was secured. Unless, of course, the residents destroyed one another, which was more of a possibility than we realized.

We continued to help the residents climb out of the hole. We helped them obtain state IDs, birth certificates, and social security cards; filled out housing paperwork; and brainstormed with all the residents how to get around the barriers they faced.

When it came time for us to meet with Smurf, he was pacing back and forth, lit with nerves, alternating between his cigarettes and the beer he had been drinking. The mental health meds he was trying weren't cutting it, due in part to his continued drinking, and his next appointment was nearly two weeks away. He was on disability benefits, but over half of that was garnished for child support. He received less than three hundred dollars a month, and his only housing options were public housing projects or a subsidized Section 8 voucher that he could use at a low-income apartment complex.

"You know I can't survive in a box," he said, clutching his can. "Even if they approve me, where am I gonna go? A place crammed in the projects with no windows, no light, no place to do my woodworking? Hell no! You know I won't make it."

At the camp, he had created a kind of sanctuary for people and animals alike. I imagined Smurf as a kind of modern-day St. Francis with hillbilly blood and Budweiser coursing through his veins. I remembered watching him nurse a baby squirrel back to health in typical Franciscan fashion. Here, he could watch the sun rise and set and tend his newly planted tomato garden. Here, he could welcome guests, provide hospitality, give gifts, and do work that made him feel valued and alive.

When we talked about his drinking, he became defensive. Any reference to detox or rehab sent him into fits of anger or tears. How long had he been self-medicating his wounds, his trauma? Would he ever make it out of the hole?

Down to the River

If I was honest, I knew that Smurf and his campmates weren't the only ones who hid their wounds and covered them over with coping mechanisms. I was still haunted by the question my grad-school teacher had asked me nearly four years before: "In all your busyness, what are you running from?"

That summer, I entered into a learning program for chaplains called Clinical Pastoral Education (CPE). I was the first street chaplain admitted to the program, and most of my colleagues served in hospitals and hospice facilities. Rumor had it that this program was demanding not only because of the long hours and assignments but also because of the emotional process I would undergo in group sessions and one-on-one sessions with my instructor. Sure enough, my wounds surfaced early. I became defensive when someone pointed out my overfunctioning, my long hours that tended toward self-destruction, and the way I bristled and pushed back when I felt like I was being criticized or boxed-in by the male instructor.

One of my assignments for CPE involved writing and presenting an autobiography to my group. While writing, I realized that guilt punctuated my family history. It was the guilt of not being able to live up to sinless perfection drilled into us in from our Church of Christ upbringing. It was the unhealthy and enmeshed family dynamic I learned from my grandparents where their guilt drove them to overfunction or overcompensate for the underfunctioning of some of our family members. It was a survivor's guilt from making it out of the wreckage of our extended family, in which suicide, mental health and addiction issues, and infidelities had fractured families. This survivor's guilt bled into my work. In the midst of the economic wreckage of our nation, I had housing, food, and health care. In my daily work of going to the shantytowns and bridges and tending wounds, I could go home, shower off the day, and sleep in my bed at night. Something in me believed I didn't deserve these comforts, so I worked myself to the bone trying to earn my worth in the eyes of others.

And there it was.

I was running from my guilt.

I was running from the guilt of imperfection, of benefitting from a system rigged in my favor, of feeling that my worth was determined by how hard I worked and what I did for others.

"You can't be a healing presence to others when you're running," said my fellow chaplain-in-training.

That summer, I visited one of the men I knew from the streets of East Nashville—John Wesley Brown, named for both the founder of Methodism and the abolitionist who led the raid on Harper's Ferry. Samuel and I had helped him move into an apartment, and he asked me what I did over the weekend. I told him I swam in the Harpeth River with Andrew and some of our friends, searched for small shells on the shore, and felt the cool waters wash over me and pull me downstream.

Two weeks later, I visited John again. He told me he was still thinking about how I swam in the river and how that filled him with hope and joy and lifted his spirits.

"You take all this too seriously," he said. His eyes reddened and glazed over as he placed his thin, weathered hand on his heart. "We can see it's wearing on you, and we need you healthy. You gotta get to that river more often, girl. Care for that soul of yours. You gotta remember how to play. When you do that for yourself, you do that for me and all of us out here."

I knew John also found solace on the river. When his parents couldn't find him at church on Sundays, they knew where to look. They'd find him on the bank, fishing pole in hand. It had been a while since John had been fishing, and it was a miracle he was still alive. He had been hospitalized and close to death multiple times over the winter; in just over a year, he too would be dead. This man knew suffering. Yet his only request for me was that I make more time to swim in rivers.

Valegia, another friend from the East Side, towered over six feet tall. "They call me Amazon," she told me when we met. We started working on her housing and frequently broke up fights between grown men together. One particularly difficult day, she pulled me aside. "I see what you're taking on," she said, "but listen here. You can't forget you're only one person. We need you out here, but you can only do so much. Sometimes you've got to put your heart in your pocket."

John, Valegia, and others saw me when I couldn't see myself, and something in me needed that. I needed their permission to take myself less seriously, to stop running from my guilt, and to let go of trying to measure my worth by how hard I worked for others. I wondered, in the words of Barbara Brown Taylor, "if my human wholeness might be more useful to God than my exhausting goodness."[4]

> "You can't forget you're only one person. We need you out here, but you can only do so much. Sometimes you've got to put your heart in your pocket."
>
> —Valegia Tidwell

That summer, as I reconnected with my love of rivers and woods, I found myself feeling more whole and able to practice what theologian Walter Brueggemann calls "Sabbath as resistance" in a culture that tells us our worth is tied up in what we produce.[5] Every Saturday or Sunday, I cleared as much of the day as I could and unplugged. I needed to learn how to give myself permission to simply be. I needed to learn how to be still while the work was unfinished, while the myriad of names and needs flooded my wandering mind. I needed to remember how to laugh and play, even when the world was on fire. So I packed my journal, an Annie Dillard book, and lunch in my bag and set off for the river or woods. And as I smelled the summer loam, listened for meadowlarks, and learned the names of wildflowers, I began to feel a little more full, a little more free.

Where Does It Hurt?

That May of 2014, the Cumberland River rose to the highest levels we'd seen since the Nashville flood of 2010. Storm systems rolled through and everyone at Smurf's riverside camp held their breath as the rains came down. The rust-brown river was roiling and reckless, but when the storms gave way, the waters retreated. The camp held.

The next week, after another long day, I got a frantic call. The floodwaters hadn't destroyed the camp and neither had the police; the residents were destroying one another. Tensions were high, nerves were frayed, words were said, and then one resident picked up a two-by-four and beat another, slamming wet wood into forehead, face, and limb.

Lauren and Samuel met me at the camp, and we started our work: survey the situation, make sure everyone is safe, tend the wounds. Two of the residents—the accuser and accused—met us on the path, but Smurf was missing. We took the wounded one first.

"How are you?" we asked the wounded one. "Where does it hurt?"

Most of the damage was internal; a concussion was definite. Soon, bruises would spread like sunset across his face and body. He refused to go to the hospital but needed somewhere safe to stay, so Lauren administered first aid and opened her home.

Then we turned to the accused, Luke, with fresh splinters in his hands, who was also wounded in ways that came through in his eyes. "What's really going on here?" we asked him. And the words and tears poured out.

"This isn't who I am," Luke said. He had learned to fight in prison. "When I was thrown into the general population, I didn't have a choice," he recounted. "It was either learn to fight or be crushed." He learned when and how to defend himself, learned that brute force meant power, and power meant survival. When he came out, he covered his wounds with drinking and women, never forgetting how it felt when a face bore a blow, when a bone snapped, never forgetting the taste, the sting, of blood.

Finally, Samuel and I found Smurf in a nearby ravine. As soon as the two-by-four came out, he had a flashback from over forty years before when his father beat him, his mother, and his siblings with fists, belts, hoses, and boards.

"If something happens," his mother would say, "run and find a ravine. I'll find you when it's over." So he ran.

Smurf was hunched, his eyes swollen and wet with tears. Samuel sat beside him and held him like a child while I took his hand in mine. The ravine was small, and we sat crumpled together on the ground. I tried to keep from shivering, shuddering, weeping, as he told us the horrors from his childhood.

Smurf's family was poor, his father ravaged by anger and addiction. He told us that one day, his father was livid at his mother. Smurf and his siblings knew something was wrong when they saw their father storming up to the house in a drunken fury, rifle in hand. Smurf's mother threw his nine-year-old body behind a mattress as bullets began to tear through windows and walls. After failed attempts to find the mother and children in the house, Smurf's father flew off toward the barn, but he stumbled and blew off part of his face. Somehow, the surgeons saved his life and reconstructed what they could. Somehow, no charges were pressed, and after a while Smurf's mother took him back.

We sat in the ravine with Smurf and held him as the dark waters of the Cumberland swirled nearby.

As the months passed and the other residents began to slowly climb up the ladder's rungs, Smurf continued to swirl around the bottom of his beer-soaked barrel. And then, on a searing summer morning, his phone rang. It was his mother calling from Upstate New York, desperate for help. She was raising his daughters and had been struggling with her own health concerns.

As Smurf recounted the call, he broke down in tears. "She's never asked me for anything all these years," he said. "So I told her okay . . . what else could I do? But then there's the other thing . . ."

"The other thing?" I asked.

"She said when I come back, I've got to be sober. She won't have me drinking in her house around the girls." He leaned down, his dirt-covered fingers sparking his lighter. The cigarette quivered in his hand. He breathed in deeply, paused, and exhaled a pillar of smoke.

For weeks, we tried every strategy to get Smurf to rehab. Samuel tried logic, tried rewiring the pathways in Smurf's mind. Didn't detox and rehab make the most sense? They would lead to a reunion with his family, a new home, a new life. Steve tried tough love. Didn't Smurf always say "Family is the most important thing"? Well, this was his chance to prove it. I tried digging into the recesses of his heart. Couldn't this plan be a balm to tend his old wounds and trauma, to reconcile, to move toward wholeness? Every now and then, we would break through the spell of addiction that held him captive. Every now and then, he would nod and cry and promise to go to rehab.

We attempted to plant seeds of sobriety and healing in Smurf's head and heart while the police continued their pressure for us to wrap things up and close the camp, once and for all.

Flames of Hell

It was now October and the song of summer cicadas was stilled. Andrew had started doctoral studies at Vanderbilt, and we had moved to the Nashville Greenlands. Our outreach team had helped to hold Smurf's camp for seven months. Most of the residents had moved into housing or rehab programs and, according to the police, the camp had to be shut down. It boiled down to property rights. Trespassing on someone else's land was a crime with consequences, a law that simply had to be enforced. The land needed to be returned to its lawful owners: a private corporation in another state that was less concerned with the "offense" than the police were. A closure date was set and agreed upon by everyone—November 10.

Smurf was the last man standing. As I traveled to South Carolina for my dad's kidney transplant, Steve helped Smurf hatch a plan with his mother. On the tenth, we would clean up the camp, pack up his belongings, and take him to detox. From there, he would go to a rehab program and then Steve would drive him and a trailer with all of his worldly possessions to Upstate New York, just in time for Christmas. Smurf agreed to the plan and prepared by selling driftwood crosses and art to save money for his new life.

When I arrived at the camp on the morning of the tenth, news cameras were already there, documenting and praising our efforts. If today went smoothly, everyone—media, volunteers, and city officials alike—would chalk this up as a win, a success. Volunteers and former residents helped disassemble the camp, heaving trash, expired canned goods, an old red armchair, and the plywood fence into a towering bonfire. This fire was powerful, angry, and unkempt. Smurf referred to it as "the fires of hell." But as I watched the flames and smoke curl above our heads, it seemed more like a lament billowing into the sky.

While the spirit of the day was somber, everyone was trying to spin a positive story. Everyone except Smurf. When everything was cleared and it was time to go, we realized he was nowhere in sight. A panic rippled through me. I checked the ravine, searched near the cars and around the back hill. Nothing. My mind raced. Some deeper instinct took over, and I let my feet carry me to the back of the camp. I found a small path that snaked toward the river, and when I climbed down the embankment, there, sitting on the roots of an old gingko tree, was Smurf. I sat on the roots beside him and we stayed there in silence. Time slowed. We watched the muddy waters swirl past our spot on the bank.

"Do you know what it's like to watch your home burn?"
—Richard "Smurf" Cole

After several minutes, he broke the silence. "Do you know what it's like to watch your home burn?" he asked. He was grief-stricken. This chapter in his life was closing, and the kingdom he built was raining down in ashes around us.

172

Finally, he got up and without a word walked back to meet the others while I followed. Conversations fell off and all eyes were on Smurf. After kicking up some dirt and ash, he made his surprise announcement. He looked down at the ground and raised his beer—his medicine—to his lips. "You can forget about rehab," he said after a swig. "I'm not doing it."

Tempers flared. "You're just going to throw everything away?" asked Steve. "What about the promises you made to us to go in today? We lined up dozens of volunteers, put ourselves out there for you, and now your beer is more important to you than us, than your mother and daughters?"

My mind spun back to the fire. Maybe Smurf was right. Maybe the fire was sheer destruction, the flames of hell. Maybe we gave in to city officials too soon. But some deeper impulse in me kicked in again. Somehow, I convinced Smurf to come have lunch with Steve and me and give it some time. He didn't have to make a decision right then. We would figure this out together.

As Smurf climbed into the car, we realized his backpack was packed with beer. Steve and I got subs for lunch, but Smurf refused to eat. When it was time to go, he refused to get in the car and, instead, marched off toward a patch of woods with his backpack.

We followed him, and Steve, who was exhausted and upset, tried the tough love thing again. He launched into the "two paths talk" about how good things would happen if Smurf chose detox and bad things would happen if he didn't. "It's your choice—take my hand and start your new life, or stay here and throw it all away." Steve reached out his hand to Smurf and held it there for a painfully long time. Smurf didn't even look up. He just stared at the ground.

"I told you," said Smurf slowly. "You can forget about the plan. I'm not going anywhere until I finish my beer."

Steve looked at me in utter disbelief. *I can't do this*, said his eyes.

"Give me a few minutes," I said, and Steve shook his head and walked away.

Smurf and I sat on the forest floor without speaking. I let the silence hold—a lesson I learned from my chaplain friends in CPE. I knew that if I tried to force anything now, it would push him away. After several minutes, he began to sob. I stayed quiet, put my hand on his shoulder. He talked about all the things he would miss from his camp: the ducks and squirrels and birds, the riverfront, waving at the barge drivers as they passed. Then he dug through his bag, pulled out a beer and cracked open the tab.

"I've got nothing," he said between sips. "Everything was taken away from me."

It was this statement and the pop of the aluminum tab that shifted something in me. "Smurf," I said firmly, leveraging six years of our friendship, "you're dealing with a lot of loss, but now is not the time for a pity party. You feel like things were taken from you? Then get off your ass and take your life back! You can do this. And you don't have to do this alone."

"I need more time," he said, his voice breaking. "I don't even know who I am."

"Let me tell you who you are," I said, looking directly at him again. "You're the talented carpenter who is more hospitable than any person I've ever met. You've taken in the sick, the elderly, the dying, and you've protected bird families and nursed baby squirrels back to health. You are loved, Smurf. You're our friend. You're a son to your mother and a father to your daughters. If you need more time, come with me now. I'm not leaving you like this. You can bring your backpack, and you can sit in my car while I go to our staff meeting. That will give you some time to think." After a couple more minutes, Smurf agreed to this proposal and walked with me up to the cars.

When Steve saw us emerging from the woods, he climbed out of his car and propped his elbow on the hood. He stared at us in awe. Smurf loaded his backpack into the car without a word.

"What kind of magic did you just pull?" Steve asked.

As planned, when Smurf finished detox, Steve picked him up. When Smurf got in the car to go to a twenty-eight-day rehab program in Kentucky, he realized he still had several cans of beer in his backpack. He stepped out of the car and pulled out the beer. Steve held his breath, fighting back a quick reaction. *Was this a mistake? Had anything changed?* Then Smurf popped open the cans one by one, and instead of drinking them, he did the unthinkable: he poured them out on the ground in the shape of a cross.

Smurf and I stayed in touch while he was in rehab, and during one of my retreats to the Abbey of Gethsemani I took him a carton of cigarettes and a photo album packed with photos from Pick-a-Tree-Village and Tent City. Twenty-eight days later, Steve took Smurf and the trailer on a road trip to upstate New York where he was reunited with his family. He moved in with his mother and his two daughters, who lived next door to his brother. Smurf and I stayed in touch, talking every few months. Years later, he would even reconnect and reconcile with his father.

"I can tell you this," he told me over the phone. "It's not a walk in the park, but I want to thank you from the bottom of my heart. You guys are the most awesomest people I've ever met. You believed in me when no one else did. And now I'm home."

11

ANOTHER WORLD

RISING UP FROM THE DEPTHS of our city stands Saint Cloud Hill, a wooded mound just south of downtown crowned by old Fort Negley—a Civil War–era stronghold built on the backs of conscripted Black laborers who helped bring down the Confederacy.

There, on a muggy summer day, I hauled my outreach backpack from the car and shut the door behind me. Samuel met me by the trail and we set off to find Chris, the "captain" of the city's largest clandestine camp.[1]

The air blazed, thick with the loamy smell of wood chips. The residents had just spread them on the mazelike trail system that led to the camp's multiple subdivisions. A passing train blew its horn and squirrels scampered through the leaves as we passed. As the trail split, we walked left to check on the residents of The Gulch, a section of the camp named, ironically, after a newly gentrified area nearby. We brought food for the older couple who had been in and out of the hospital. We caught up with the twentysomethings at Ninja Capitol who had scrawled in huge black letters on one of their tents, "1234 Dirt Ln., Anywhere U.S.A." We snaked up another trail to the camp of a couple who had hand-laid hundreds of stones into three intricate firepits. "Welcome Home" read a large flat stone propped against the first flame-licked pit.

We walked over to the trail that branched to the right of the main path and hit the Rabbit Hole, Far Point Station, and Plantation Point, checking in with whoever was home. Then we climbed up to the Kingdom of God camp at the top of the hill that boasted a stunning view of downtown. Almost every subdivision was well maintained and each tent was hoisted off the ground by the signature pallet decks built by Captain Chris. From there, we cut down to Chris's neatly groomed camp. A hand-painted sign reading "Eagle's Nest Landing" was nailed to a tree above our heads, and his battery-powered radio blasted country-rock. He was hammering away.

The day before, police had come through the camp. They said the residents had to be out by September 15. But this wasn't the first time the city had tried to close this camp.

The first time I met Chris was in the winter of 2009. He was a vendor and writer for *The Contributor*. Andrew worked closely with Chris and remembers the day he burst into their weekly paper release meeting, utterly distraught. It was his birthday and he had just lost everything. "They took it all: my tent, my Bible, my world!" he cried, his thick New York accent harried in fits and starts.

In the heart of winter, without warning, police officers had dragged his tent, filled with his belongings, and several other tents down the hill and threw them away. Did the officers bring a public works dumpster to haul them off or load them into a truck? Was it Metro police? Parks police? It didn't matter. They took everything. The land was owned by Metro Parks, and the residents were participating in unauthorized and unlawful camping. We helped Chris with blankets, another tent, and a Bible. And he rebuilt.

In 2014, the city tried to close the camp again under Mayor Dean. Our scrappy outreach team from Open Table Nashville, fresh from defending Smurf's campsite, stepped in and helped the residents organize. Media pressure was enough to hold off city officials then. But now, a year later, they were back, and another mayoral campaign was underway, promising new leadership.

As Samuel and I walked into Eagle's Nest Landing, Chris kept hammering. Despite the eviction notice, he was still building. He was bent over on the ground, cigarette hanging from his lips, pounding the last plank into place. Chris was a poet and song-writer who had battled his own addictions and moved to Tennessee for a fresh start. Chris was one of the hardest-working men I'd ever met. For years, he'd been dragging pallets up to the camp, prying the boards apart, and then nailing them tightly back in place. He placed each refinished pallet beside another until they stretched into impressive decks large enough for massive tents and covered seating areas.

When he finished, he greeted us with a sweaty hug and slicked his sandy-brown hair into a ponytail. "They'll come around," he said. "They'll see this is part of the solution." Samuel and I didn't have the same faith in city officials but admired Chris's determination. "We're giving people a place to start here," he continued. "A place to get off the streets, to get sober, to be in nature, to turn things around. I've seen people get off drugs out here, get into housing. And it's all because they had somewhere to start, people to care."

> "We're giving people a place to start here, a place to get off the streets, to get sober, to be in nature, to turn things around."
> —Captain Chris Scott Fieselman

A few minutes later, we heard another camp resident raving as he made his way down the trail. "Here's what I'm gonna do," he shouted. It was Dewayne. He was shirtless in the heat, and his coffee-colored skin beaded with sweat. "I'm gonna take this through the courts. And I don't want any help from your legal people. God's hand is gonna guide this.

The Bible says we've got to submit ourselves to our government so that's what I'm gonna do."

This caught my attention. It seemed contradictory for Dewayne to willingly break the law and then give himself over to the mercy of the very same law.

"Does God ask us to submit ourselves to unjust governments and laws?" I asked. Dewayne paused and I continued. "You know, there's some talk of submission in the Bible, but there's also talk of civil disobedience." I told him that some scholars said that the first instance of civil disobedience in the Bible could be found in Exodus when the Hebrew midwives disobeyed Pharaoh's orders to kill all the baby boys. Dewayne smiled.

"You know, you're alright," he said, granting his approval not just to the idea but also to me. "It's like sometimes we follow the rules, but if the rules are messed up, God helps us decide when to break them."

"Exactly," I said with a grin. I reminded him that we still had legal support available, and he said he'd consider it. Maybe.

Just Like That

The next morning, camp residents awoke to the revving of city chainsaws and the rumble of bobcats coming up the hill. Samuel and I rushed to the scene and called local reporters. Monstrous metal teeth tore through the lower levels of the camp, clearing branches and trees and widening the main trail so bulldozers could pass through.

The larger bulldozers didn't come that day, and neither did the police. But they would. And the message was clear: *This is not your land. This is not your home. We can take away everything you've built just like that.*

"This is a modern-day land struggle," I told the press. "What you're seeing here today is an age-old battle."

As the September deadline neared, service providers and out-reach groups from across the city came together to work with the residents on housing. But the waiting lists were long. And even our friends who received Section 8 vouchers were struggling to find openings at low-income apartment complexes. As Nashville grew, the rents skyrocketed, metal cranes twisted in the sky, and the affordable housing crisis deepened. We continued to help the residents hold camp meetings and "Know Your Rights" sessions with Tripp, the attorney. If Metro cleared the camp, many of the people on the hill had nowhere to legally exist. How could Metro cite and arrest them without providing other legal options?

A parks board meeting was held early in September, and I joined Samuel, Ingrid, several camp residents, and nearly two dozen advocates as we packed the room and lined our backs against the walls. The board meeting was business as usual, and when it was clear that they weren't going to discuss the impending closure of the camp, Ingrid eyed me from across the room. *You ready?* she mouthed, eyebrows raised. I nodded. We walked up to the middle of the room with two residents from the camp and interrupted the meeting. The room fell silent and my heart pounded as the news cameras turned on us.

"I'm sorry," stammered one of the parks board members, "we're not taking public comments at this time."

Ingrid cleared her throat. "I understand," she said, "but while your job is to get through this agenda, my job as an advocate is to speak out when something isn't right. So I'm asking you to hear us out."

We held the room for fifteen minutes. Residents spoke passionately about their daily struggles and lack of options. Ingrid and I spoke about the lack of affordable housing and how moving folks off park land meant they would just move to other outlawed camps. The director of parks cited safety concerns and police calls from the area. We argued that when a neighborhood has an issue, you don't evict the entire block; rather, you deal with the issue at hand.

"This is certainly complex," said the director, "but allowing the camp to stay is not the answer. If we don't uphold our responsibilities as Parks and Recreation, it opens the city up to liability issues." The director and board members agreed to come back to the issue the next week and talk to other Metro departments.

The deadline passed, a few citations were handed out that were ultimately retired, and a new mayor, Megan Barry, was voted in and installed. Many referred to Barry as a "homeless-friendly" mayor because she had served on the Homelessness Commission. She gave the camp a reprieve until April 15 and convened an Encampment Task Force that would begin meeting in the new year. I was appointed to serve on the task force along with Charlie, my mentor; a former Tent City resident named Wendell; and half a dozen others. We had some breathing room but still no idea how it would all end. While we worked toward a larger solution and the city considered arguments for the creation of a sanctioned campsite, we collaborated with other service providers to house as many of the residents as we could.

"Fight Like Hell"

The coolness of autumn came and went, the camp stayed intact, and then another brutal winter set in. That winter, the death toll climbed. In one week alone, I lost four of the people I worked with. One man was beaten on the side of the road. Another was beaten and burned beyond recognition. A musician I worked with froze to death in his tent, and one of the women I had recently housed was found dead in her apartment. Then, one bitter night, my coworkers and I convinced two men to come in from the cold who barely made it. Plum-black clouds billowed up their feet and legs. Both were hospitalized. One lost several toes. The other lost both his feet. It was all too much.

Those who think homelessness is a choice haven't seen the carnage up close.

"I was always told that hell came after death," one man on the streets told me, "but I think hell is here, on earth."

There were nights I collapsed into sobs as Andrew held me. There were mornings I woke before the sun, shaken by the ghosts who visited me, whispering of worlds past and worlds to come.

"Pray for the dead," said Mother Jones, "and fight like hell for the living."[2] So we did. We held memorials to honor our friends. We tended wounds. And we channeled the grief and urgency we felt into trying to create another world.

As the trauma of February melted into March, weekly task force meetings were held and more advocates began attending. Frustration was building that there were still no solutions for the camp. The April 15 deadline held. I brought proposals to the meetings for the creation of sanctioned camps, but the board voted against them. Charlie, Wendell, and I were outnumbered.

"Creating more *housing* is the solution," said one task force member, "not more encampments."

"Of course!" I said, incensed. "But people have to have somewhere to legally exist until that housing is available."

One of the only tangible results to come out of the task force was a proposal I brought that our team at Open Table had been researching. We proposed that the city create a homeless outreach team under Metro that could serve as a liaison between campsites and the police. Homelessness was an economic and social services issue, we argued, *not* a criminal one. Within a year, this proposal had funding, and guidelines were created for working with encampments slated for closure. Gone were the days when the city cleared camps without notice. At least we hoped.

But was it enough to save the camp at Fort Negley?

One of the bright spots during that season was the return of Ray, my old friend who was part of Hobson House, Occupy, and the housing rights group. Ray had spent the past couple years locked up in Georgia on an old charge, and we had kept in touch through writing letters. As soon as he was out, he moved back to Nashville and set up a new camp near a rock quarry. When Ray heard about the closure of Fort Negley, he wanted to get involved.

"We've got to band together," Ray said, "show some solidarity across camps. Today they're coming for Negley, but how long before they come for us?"

Others on the street started mobilizing as well, trying to do what they could to support each other. A man we had helped house from Tent City called me one afternoon. "I saw the news report about Fort Negley," he said. "You can bring some of 'em to my place. They can use my bed and I'll sleep on the couch. I know what it's like not to have one."

We held camp meetings around Chris's firepit at Eagle's Nest Landing and brought pizza for the residents. "What's gonna happen on the fifteenth?" one asked. "I can't afford to be arrested, but where else are we gonna go?"

"I ain't got no choice," said another resident. "At least if I go to jail, I'll have somewhere to sleep."

What could we tell them? We had no idea what to expect, but we knew that city officials were not toying around. Why was Mayor Barry moving forward with this? She wasn't a bad person and was getting terrible press—the pending camp closure was making national news. Didn't she understand our predicament? Then, a few days before the deadline, Barry held a press conference and pledged ten million dollars for our local affordable housing trust fund. The occasion was momentous, but the timing felt disingenuous. If she cared so much, why close the camp? What were we missing?

"We don't know what's going to happen," I said to the residents as the campfire flashed against the night. "But we can promise you that we'll stand beside you and fight this with you. If they arrest you, they arrest us." This was a familiar promise—one that we had made before and would make again—and we meant it. While the end results were out of our control, we knew that this solidarity, this accompaniment, mattered.

More meetings followed with campers, advocates, and organizers. A copwatch was established on the hill, with volunteers rotating nights, and we began planning for our own press conference and rally at city hall on April 15. We had two demands for our city's leaders: first, end the criminalization of homelessness, halting all camp closures until viable alternatives were found, and second, commit to creating a comprehensive and strategic plan to address the staggering need for affordable housing. The event would culminate with a march and sleep-out at the fort.

Praying with Our Feet

The fifteenth of April brought a powerful panoply of images. The sprawling lawn of city hall dotted with a dozen tents and a hundred protest signs. Late afternoon light glinting off the fountain's spray. A sea of people under a crisp cerulean sky. Folks who were unhoused from Fort Negley and across the city. Outreach workers and housing advocates. Labor unions and the lawyers guild. Students and professors. Moms with strollers. Activists from Black Lives Matter and immigrant and refugee rights groups. Latinx and Puerto Rican organizers. Former occupiers, Tent City residents, and members of the Power Project. Andrew, my love. Our college friend Richard who had helped us plan our first rally on the same lawn. My coworkers from Open Table Nashville and their families. My heart soared.

"You showed up for our people," my union friend told me, "and now we're showing up for yours."

I thought of my first rally on the same lawn nearly ten years earlier. The cherry trees in bloom, the nerves that rocked me, the commitments we made, the commitments we kept. I looked around at the people I had marched beside so many times over the years and a tide of gratitude, awe, and belonging rose in my chest.

If hell was here on earth, so was heaven, and it opened around us, within us. "Another world is not only possible," said author Arundhati Roy, "she is on her way. On a quiet day, I can hear her breathing."[3] So I listened as her whispers whipped around us on the cool April breeze.

The press conference and rally were impassioned, commanding, electric. Sparks flew and lit something fierce in us. We set off on the two-mile march to Fort Negley, praying with our feet all the way as the dusk deepened into night. Children marched with their parents and we waved the yellow flags of justice and hoisted tents above our heads like the ark of the covenant. Andrew carried an orange protest sign cut into the shape of a key that read "House Keys Not Handcuffs." Ray's voice rose above the rest, leading the chants we had practiced. "Nashville, stand up and fight! Housing is a human right!" he shouted. Someone beat a bucket like a drum, and the city lights blinked on, bearing witness to our holy procession.

Our chanting grew louder as we approached the camp, and the residents who stayed on the hill wandered down with teary eyes and mouths agape. We enveloped the residents in hugs and gathered for a handful of speeches. Chris greeted the crowd, thanking everyone for coming out. "We did good tonight," he said, welling up as he looked around.

The attorneys told the crowd what to do if the police came to cite or arrest us. "Now, we've been talking to the district attorney's office," said one attorney from beneath his neon green legal observer hat, "and they don't have any interest in prosecuting any charges that come from this. National cases have set the precedent that people shouldn't be charged when they have nowhere else to go. Unfortunately, that might not stop the cops."

When the pizza came, we broke bread together, and then began to set up camp for the night. This was a sleep-out. If the police came, we'd be there.

It was just after midnight when four officers with flashlights walked up. *No zip-tie cuffs*, I noted as they walked by. Cameras were rolling and they were cordial. Chris, ever the host, always trying to win city officials over, welcomed them and guided them up the hill. They took the names of all camp residents, checked their IDs, and handed out more paper notices stating that the camp would still be closed. Some of us offered our names and IDs in solidarity, but it was clear the officers came only for the residents.

We woke up the next morning to breakfast brought by our friends from the Nashville chapter of Black Lives Matter. The previous year, we had shown solidarity to many of the lead organizers and supported their actions. We had attended their vigils, helped with safety at demonstrations, and marched alongside them after the nonindictment verdicts for the police officers who murdered Mike Brown and Eric Garner. We formed deep friendships and knew that the struggle for racial justice was intertwined with the struggle for housing justice. They brought orange juice, coffee, muffins, bagels—the works. We greeted each other with hugs and one of the residents took them on a tour of the remnants of the camp.

After the next day had passed, however, officers came back in the middle of the night, waking the residents and checking their IDs. The next night was the same, and on the third night, citations were handed out. The citations amounted to no more than scare tactics to get the residents to move on. If the charges were argued in court, the residents and our attorneys would likely win. In the end, the city would retire the charges, denying Chris and others the chance to argue their case. But something worse than citations was coming.

The next morning, the sound of mechanical thunder roared over the hill, and the campers' world was turned upside down. This time, city employees hadn't come with just chainsaws and bobcats. They brought bulldozers and massive dumpsters. They plowed through the trails. Chainsaws chewed through pallet decks, and the bulldozers pulled debris and empty tents down the hill to the dumpster. Behemoth machines barreled into occupied camps and crushed through the brush around them. The crack and cascade of falling trees echoed across the hill. Samuel and I arrived as soon as we got the call and held the residents as they shook and wept.

After the police left, we surveyed the damage. It was as if a tornado had torn through the hill, touching down here and there.

But this disaster was no act of God. This terror was man-made, and more would come. Absent were the people in power who made the decisions. They weren't there to see the trauma and wreckage. They never were.

"They don't hear the birds sing in the early morning," said Chris. "They don't hear the whip-poor-wills cry after sunset. They don't see the bats fly against the night sky. They don't know what they're destroying."

I remembered from childhood the clothesline and patch of woods downhill from our church that was mowed down. I thought of my grandfather, a highly revered developer, who cleared over a thousand acres of former cotton fields and Carolina woods to make way for two mammoth subdivisions. I thought of how he "moved along the former Negro sharecroppers" who were squatting in shanties on the land he purchased. I remembered hearing stories about how family members and friends helped dig out a man-made lake with bobcats. These stories were told over Thanksgiving dinners and family meals without a second thought. While some squatters were allowed to stay on the land for a time, who was there to stand with the displaced? Where did they go?

I remembered being five years old and wandering through the woods with my grandmother, brother, and cousins. We were going to the creek but could hear the rumble of bulldozers in the distance and smell the freshly poured asphalt wafting on the breeze. Those woods would soon be teeming with houses, cul-de-sacs, tennis courts, and a pool.

My grandparents on my mother's side came from different worlds, and both their histories swam in me. My grandfather grew up on a small farm, and he and his siblings worked their way into the upper crust of Alabama society. He was as religious and respectable as they come—one of the first elders of our church and a conscientious objector and medic during World War II. My grandfather and his brother, both developers and businessmen, built their wealth, in part, by capitalizing on the commodification of land that was first stolen from indigenous communities. I never heard anyone from our family or church talk about the ethics of development and displacement, despite the mandate in Scripture to care for the poor. This was just the way it was.

My grandmother grew up as the dirt-poor daughter of a coal miner in Appalachia whose brothers and father died of black lung. She was a folk artist whose longing for wild things and independence blazed in her as fiercely as her once-red hair. My histories simmered in me. There's nothing we can do to change our past or the lives that precede us. Still, we must reckon with our roots, make amends wherever possible, and decide which side we're on.

Back at the camp, service providers who were working with city officials urged the residents to leave, offering the concession of hotel vouchers to sweeten the deal. If the stick didn't work, use the carrot. And most of the residents whose spirits were already pummeled by the stick went for the carrot. A handful of folks remained on the hill for a few more weeks until the police and bulldozers came back one final time. And this time they didn't just clear out the brush. They flattened every firepit and ripped out every tent and pallet deck. All in all, they ravaged eleven acres of forest, stripping the entire hill nearly bare. When they finished, Saint Cloud Hill looked as if the flames of hell had utterly charred it, leaving only a handful of scattered trees. Metro Parks and the mayor's office provided no explanation for the clearing, but in a few months' time we would learn that they were taking development bids for the adjacent property—prime real estate a stone's throw away from downtown.

Not the Enemy

At the end of the day, however, what left me in awe was not the violence of our city and a "homeless-friendly" mayor. It was the residents' resilience, their ability to go on. "Some seeds germinate best after a fire," I once read. And germinate they did. Chris searched for more land to rebuild. Housing vouchers came through for some of the residents, and they moved into apartments across town. Ray and some of the others from the camp started attending meetings that would lead to the formation of one of the most powerful tenants' rights groups Nashville has ever seen.

One morning in May, I called up a few of the residents. I heard that some of the immigrant rights activists who had come to city hall to support the camp residents were organizing a protest of their own. New Immigration and Customs Enforcement raids had just been announced at a national level, targeting undocumented women and children. The man responsible for carrying out such decisions, the secretary of Homeland Security, just happened to be the keynote speaker at a local high school's graduation ceremony.

"I'm going to support," I told the former camp residents. "Wanna join?" Four of us drove to the protest together, windows down.

"You know," said one of the men from the back, "I hear people on the worksite talking all the time about how the immigrants come over here and steal our jobs. But they're just like us, fighting for a better life. They don't deserve to have their homes raided. We know what that's like."

"Yeah," said another, "they're not the enemy. It's the system. It's greed. It's the people in power who set us against each other and pay us next to nothing."

I smiled from the front seat, my hair dancing through the breeze. What would happen if we all came together to channel our collective anger, energy, and love?

"We cannot say," wrote Brazilian educator Paulo Freire, "that in the process of revolution someone liberates someone else . . . but rather that people in communion liberate each other."[4]

Always Down

"What keeps you going?" asked one of our interns after another long week of outreach work. I answered with a half-hearted quip about hope—something true, but unconvincing and feeble.

What I should have said, in a hushed voice as I leaned forward, was this: love.

Love that fills me when I'm hollow and carries me when I can't make it another step. A love that accompanies, that freely gives and graciously receives. A love that shares its tent, its hoodie, and its warmest quilt.

Love is the most powerful force on earth when wielded by those who realize that our liberation is bound up together; who pray with our hands, tears, fury, and feet; who keep the candles and campfires of resistance burning through the darkest nights of oppression.

Love draws us down, flowing like water to the lowest point. We find the valleys wherever we go. Who dwells there in the valley? People without houses. People locked in cages. People who are weary and cast out. People who don't fit into our boxes. Love drives us to them, always. Once reluctant, now convicted, we leave our pockets of comfort and power where trouble seems so far away. We descend with the mountain-moving force of a never-failing stream, carving out canyons and wearing away rocks that once felt immovable. Like so many who have gone before us, we swim in the sacred sea of the people. It is in the valley, in the river, in the shadows, always, that we find our God. It is here that we keep believing, against all odds, that another world is not only possible but that it is on its way. And maybe, just maybe, it is already here—breathing our breath, sprouting like seed.

> *Love is the most powerful force on earth when wielded by those who realize that our liberation is bound up together.*

EPILOGUE

THIS MORNING, Andrew and I awoke to a frenzy of feathers on glass. Behind our linen curtains, we saw the dark silhouette of a bird beating its wings against the window for what seemed like minutes. Its presence left me rattled and stirred something in me. Was it the canary in the mine? The raven that couldn't find land after the flood of Noah's time? Or the dove that did find land, carrying the olive leaf of a new world?

I am writing these words on Palm Sunday from a world that is, in many ways, remarkably different from the one captured in these pages. As I write, COVID-19 is ravaging the country and globe. Soon after this, worldwide uprisings for racial justice would ignite, toppling the statues of Confederates and colonizers and calling for justice for Ahmaud Arbery, Breonna Taylor, George Floyd, and other Black victims of white supremacy and police brutality.

To add to the upheaval, just two weeks before the local quarantine orders hit and during my fifth month of pregnancy, an EF3 tornado tore through Nashville, destroying our home, our neighborhood, and a large swath of our city.

"Do you know what it's like to watch your home burn?" I remember Smurf asking so many years before. I shook my head then, but now I have a deeper understanding.

We are learning the grief of disaster and displacement in new and stunning ways. But we are also learning the gift of grace and solidarity as well—the hands that pick up the pieces with you, prepare food for you, and welcome you into their homes. The first person to show up at our mangled house to help us salvage what we could was Raphael, a friend I'd met at Tent City over a decade ago. We accompany others and find ourselves supported in return.

And so today, on Palm Sunday of 2020, as irises bloom and billions of people across the earth are scattered and ordered to stay home, even when they have no home in which to dwell, I'm thinking about what it means to ride a donkey instead of a war horse. I'm thinking about the tables of exploitation that will be overturned, the feet that will be washed, the bread and bodies that will be broken, and what will rise from the ashes.

I am writing these words in a season of apocalypse—a time of unveiling in which the old world is dying and a new world is trying to be born. What will emerge from these present crises? Was the bird a canary, a raven, or a dove?

ACKNOWLEDGMENTS

I FEEL LIKE MY HEART is physically expanding with gratitude when I think about all the people who have accompanied me over the years: those who encouraged me when I was at my wit's end, believed in me when I doubted myself, and taught me that my wholeness matters too. This work and the stories herein are the work of a community—not an individual—and I am honored to live among so many fierce and kindred spirits.

First, my deepest gratitude to Andrew. Andrew, my love, your partnership has both grounded and balanced me. Our marriage has been a shelter from the storm, and I feel endlessly thankful to have married my best friend, who shares my deepest commitments and just so happens to be an exceptional writer and editor too. You are patient with me, love me even when I'm a mess (which is often), and have spent so much time helping me sharpen these stories. It is a joy to live by your side, and I can't wait to nurture a family together and grow into these next chapters of life with you.

My deepest gratitude, also, to our family. To my parents, for teaching me how to live with integrity and advocate for the underdog, and for your unconditional love and support over the years. To my dearest sister, Ansley, who grew up in the midst of these events, for your friendship, your heart, your loving support, and all of our talks and walks together. To my brother, Russell, for your friendship, for always keeping things exciting and unpredictable, and for your desire to live life fully. To Greg and Linda Krinks and the stunning family of love I married into, for your ceaseless encouragement and unfailing support.

Next, my heartfelt thanks to my mentors who "lived the questions" before me and whose lives, voices, and examples guide me still. To Charlie Strobel, for extending your hand of support and guidance so early in my journey and for your continued accompaniment. To Scott Owings, for introducing Andrew and me to contemplative spirituality and for being a consistent and centering presence in our lives for so long. To Judy Beisswenger and the late Don Beisswenger, for your beautiful lives and for the ways you've loved, supported, and encouraged us over the years. To Karl Meyer and Pam Beziat at the Nashville Greenlands, for the community you've created and welcomed us into and for your inspiring and long-standing commitment to simplicity, resistance, and sustainability. To my mentors and friends from the Nashville Homeless Power Project, specifically Clemmie Greenlee, Madge Johnson, Howard Allen, Cathie Buckner, Matt Leber, and Garret Stark, for taking me under your wings and continuing to fight the good fight.

I offer all my love to my closest friends and comrades. We've been through hell and back together, and I can't imagine this journey without you. To Jeannie Alexander, my spirit sister, for your fierce love, your fire, and your friendship. To Lauren Plummer, my dearest friend, for sharing every inch of life together through countless highs and lows, for your abiding commitment to the struggle, and for your radical care and creativity. To Ingrid McIntyre, for encouraging me to care for myself and for the energy and untamed love you bring to this work. To Brett Flener, for the ways you show up, and to Richard Harper, for teaching me how to love a city. To all my dear friends who have worked with us at Open Table Nashville over the years (and all our volunteers, interns, board members, and supporters), specifically Samuel Lester, Haley

Spigner, Linda Bailey, Lisa Avrit, Susan Adcock, Andre Chunaco, Allie Wallace, Susannah Shumate, Liz Shadbolt, Autumn Dennis, Jenna Wisler, Becca Dryden, Elizabeth Langgle-Martin, Steve Lindstrom, Caleigh Keadle, Jennifer Bailey, Sabrina Sullenberger, Randy Goodman, and so many others—your love, support, and camaraderie keep me going. To my friends from Tent City and other encampments and alleys across Nashville, specifically Richard "Smurf" Cole, Teresa Gordon, Stacey Farley, Michael "Bama" Farley, Wendell Segroves, Reginald "Vegas" Watson, Raphael McPherson, Ray Telford, Chris Scott Fieselman, Valegia Tidwell, Brian Jones, the East Nashville crew, and others—you have taught me more about love, resilience, and radical hospitality than any story could ever convey. To my friends who are incarcerated, for your perseverance and support. To the attorneys who have so graciously represented us and our friends on the streets, specifically Tripp Hunt, Mike Engle, Will York, and Chad Hindman. To my friends in the movement community, both near and far, and my friends in Nashville's homeless outreach community and at Park Center, including Will Connelly, Judy Tackett, Laurie Green, Lauren Russell, and so many others, for your grit, determination, and disruptive love. To Jace Freeman and Sean Clark—The Moving Picture Boys—who filmed and documented so many of the events in this book with such artistry and care.

I am eternally thankful to the universities and professors who helped form me and to the faith communities who have supported and journeyed alongside Open Table Nashville over the years. To everyone at Lipscomb University who encouraged and challenged Andrew and me. To Lee Camp, Matt Hearn, Richard Goode, Dana and Greg Carpenter, and so many others who taught us to think critically and inspired us to pursue justice. To everyone at Vanderbilt Divinity School who embraced Andrew and me from day one. To Melissa Snarr, Dan Joranko, Viki Matson, Trudy Stringer, Bruce Morrill, Emilie Townes, and so many others who deepened my theology, offered a space for me to bring my whole self, and opened doors for me to pioneer a new kind of ministry on the streets of Nashville. To Acklen Church of Christ, for being so steadfast in your support of my ministry and our work over the years and for the ways you've welcomed me into your community. To Green Street Church—to Caleb Pickering, Russ Arnold, and others—for always saying "yes" when possible and continuing to show the world what a tiny church with great love can do. To the host of Methodist churches and the Tennessee Conference of United Methodist Churches who have provided a stable foundation for our work and have been so unwavering in your support of Open Table Nashville from the beginning. To our dear friends at Otter Creek Church who have remained part of our community. To everyone at the Abbey of Gethsemani for "welcoming the stranger as Christ" and offering a space of centering, silence, and retreat to people like me in the midst of a noisy and chaotic world.

And finally, my sincerest thanks to my agent, Angela Scheff with The Christopher Ferebee Agency, who believed in this project early on, and to my editors, Katelyn Beaty and Julie Zahm, along with others at Brazos Press who took a chance on me and helped this project come to fruition. Getting to know you all and work with you has been an honor and a joy. To my dear friend Michael McRay, who has helped me navigate so much of the writing and publishing world and has been so generous in helping me make connections. To Robyn Henderson-Espinoza, for your encouragement and solidarity. To my incredible writing group—Anna Reid, Diana Johnson, Towles Kintz, Lara Apgar, and Katie McDougall, cofounder of The Porch Writing Collective—who read so much of my early manuscript and helped me hone the stories and images herein. And to Kelsey Cobbs, my friend and former intern at Open Table Nashville, for your tireless resolve in helping me track down the sources of so many quotes for this book.

All my love. All my thanks. Let's keep praying with our feet and building a better world together!

NOTES

Author's Note

1. "The General Thanksgiving," *The Book of Common Prayer* (New York: Church Publishing Incorporated, 2007), 59.

Chapter 1: Upstream

1. For more recent statistics about global poverty and hunger, visit The Hunger Project's website at https://www.thp.org/knowledge-center/know-your-world -facts-about-hunger-poverty.

2. William Stafford, "A Ritual to Read to Each Other," in *The Way It Is: New and Selected Poems* (St. Paul: Graywolf Press, 1998), 136.

3. Flannery O'Connor, *Mystery and Manners: Occasional Prose*, ed. Sally Fitzgerald and Robert Fitzgerald (New York: Farrar, Straus & Giroux, 1969), 34.

4. Uma Majmudar, *Gandhi's Pilgrimage of Faith: From Darkness to Light* (Albany: State University of New York Press, 2005), 71.

5. One of my friends from the Power Project once told me, "We're not home-less—we're unhoused. We make a home wherever we can. What we lack is adequate housing." I use "unhoused" throughout this book in honor of that sentiment. I also seek to use person-centered language that focuses on the individual person instead of the condition they are experiencing.

Chapter 2: Descent

1. Dorothy Day, *The Long Loneliness* (New York: Harper & Row, 1952), 45.

2. Day, *Long Loneliness*, 59.

3. Quoted in Geoff Foster, Carol Levine, and John Williamson, *A Generation at Risk: The Global Impact of HIV/AIDS on Orphans and Vulnerable Children* (Cambridge: Cambridge University Press, 2006), 159.

4. Day, *Long Loneliness*, 39.

5. Day, *Long Loneliness*, 216.

6. Banksy, *Wall and Piece* (London: Century, 2005), 52.

7. The Rutba House, *School(s) for Conversion: 12 Marks of a New Monasticism* (Eugene, OR: Cascade Books, 2005), 10.

8. For more, see Lindsey German and John Rees, *A People's History of London* (London: Verso, 2012).

9. Joe Hill, "The Preacher and the Slave," *The Little Red Song Book*, international edition (Ypsilanti, MI: Industrial Workers of the World, 1995), 49.

Chapter 3: Broken Soil

1. Robert Coles, *Dorothy Day: A Radical Devotion* (New York: Perseus Books, 1999), 134.

2. Thomas Merton, *A Book of Hours*, ed. Kathleen Deignan (Notre Dame, IN: Sorin Books, 2007), 98.

3. In 2018 Monsanto was acquired by Bayer, one of the largest pharmaceutical companies in the world. In the early twentieth century, Bayer merged with other companies to create IG Farben, a pharmaceutical conglomerate that conducted medical experiments on prisoners in concentration camps and used slave labor during the Holocaust.

4. C. Lugo, "Homeless Occupy HUD House in Nashville," May 7, 2008, https://www.youtube.com/watch?v=a_gmO5bbYRQ.

5. Steve Samra, "New Leader Alexander Calls for Year of Jubilee," *The Contributor*, June 2008.

Chapter 4: Downhill

1. Donal Dorr, *The Social Justice Agenda: Justice, Ecology, Power, and the Church* (New York: Orbis Books, 1991), 126.

2. Jeannie Alexander, "The Littlest Bum." *The Contributor*, March 2009.

3. More information can be found at the website for the National Coalition for the Homeless, https://www.nationalhomeless.org/factsheets/families.html.

4. Parker Palmer, "The Gift of Presence, the Perils of Advice," *On Being*, April 27, 2016, https://onbeing.org/blog/the-gift-of-presence-the-perils-of-advice.

5. This approach has striking similarities to Trauma-Informed Care, a widely recognized evidence-based practice developed in recent years.

Chapter 5: Burning Hearts

1. Mark Lewis Taylor, *The Executed God: The Way of the Cross in Lockdown America*, 2nd ed. (Minneapolis: Fortress, 2015), 33.

Chapter 6: Wilderness

1. Many of the events in this section are depicted in the documentary *Tent City, U.S.A.*, directed by Steven Cantor, originally aired April 5, 2012, on Oprah Winfrey Network (OWN). This documentary is available to purchase and watch online.

2. Beard's words are documented and in Jeannie Alexander, "Closing the Gates of Charity," *The Contributor*, July 2010.

3. Alexander, "Closing the Gates of Charity."

4. Redlining is the practice of withholding bank loans and other resources from predominantly Black neighborhoods.

5. Bill Moyers, foreword to Jim Wallis, *Faith Works: From the Life of an Activist Preacher* (New York: Random House, 2000), xvii.

Chapter 7: Emergence

1. Joseph Stilglitz, "Of the 1%, By the 1%, For the 1%," *Vanity Fair*, May 2011, https://www.vanityfair.com/news/2011/05/top-one-percent-201105.

2. Dorothee Soelle, *The Strength of the Weak: Toward a Christian Feminist Identity* (Philadelphia: Westminster, 1984), 155.

3. Walter Brueggemann, foreword to Stanley P. Saunders and Charles L. Campbell, *The Word on the Street: Performing the Scriptures in the Urban Context* (Eugene, OR: Wipf & Stock, 2000), xii.

4. Quoted in the introduction to *Dom Helder Camara: Essential Writings*, ed. Francis McDonagh (Maryknoll: Orbis Books, 2009), 11.

5. Slavoj Zizek, "Zizek at Occupy Wall Street," transcript by Ippolit Belinski, Zizek.uk, November 9, 2016, https://zizek.uk/zizek-at-occupy-wall-street-transcript/.

Chapter 8: Accompaniment

1. In August of 2020 Tennessee lawmakers amended this law to make these nonviolent "offenses" a felony punishable with a sentence of up to six years in prison and the loss of voting rights.

2. The eviction of Occupy Nashville is chronicled in a short documentary titled *HB 2638/SB 2508 - March 8, 2012 - An Installment of the Nashville Docujournal Series* by The Moving Picture Boys, available at http://www.docujournal.com/campinglaw. Another short documentary that captures the one-year anniversary gathering for Occupy Nashville, where housing rights are discussed, is titled *Occupy Anniversary - October Anniversary - An Installment of the Docujournal Series* by The Moving Picture Boys, available at https://www.youtube.com/watch?v=vGDRWoM28YE.

3. Dorothee Soelle, *Suffering* (Philadelphia: Fortress, 1975), 177.

4. Rainer Maria Rilke, *Letters to a Young Poet* (New York: Norton, 1954), 27.

5. "Report on the Situation of Human Rights in El Salvador," Inter-American Commission on Human Rights, November 17, 1978, https://www.cidh.oas.org/countryrep/ElSalvador78eng/chap.2.htm.

6. James R. Brockman, *Romero: A Life* (Maryknoll: Orbis Books, 2005), 78.

7. Brockman, *Romero*, 81.

8. For more information about St. Martin of Tours, the legend of the cloak, and the etymology of the word "chaplain," see https://www.britannica.com/biography/Saint-Martin-of-Tours and https://www.britannica.com/topic/chapel.

Chapter 9: Wick

1. The public funeral march for Jimmy Fulmer is depicted in the short documentary titled *Nashville Docujournal: Homeless Funeral Procession - January 18,*

2013 by The Moving Picture Boys, available at http://www.docujournal.com/homeless.

2. Mary Beth Rogers, *Cold Anger: A Story of Faith and Power Politics* (Denton, TX: University of North Texas Press, 1990).

3. Thomas Merton, "In Silence," in *The Collected Poems of Thomas Merton* (New York: New Directions, 1980), 280–81.

4. Mary Oliver, "What I Have Learned So Far," in *New and Selected Poems* (Boston: Beacon, 2005), 2:57.

5. I first heard the horizon analogy from liberation theologian Gustavo Gutierrez. He writes about what he calls the "salvific horizon" and "eschatological horizon" in his book *A Theology of Liberation: History, Politics, and Salvation* (Maryknoll, NY: Orbis Books, 1973).

Chapter 10: Tending Wounds

1. For further reading and statistics, see Terry Gross, "A 'Forgotten History' of How the U.S. Government Segregated America," Fresh Air on NPR, May 3, 2017, https://www.npr.org/2017/05/03/526655831/a-forgotten-history-of-how-the-u-s-government-segregated-america, and Richard Rothstein, *The Color of Law: A Forgotten History of How Our Government Segregated America* (New York: Liveright, 2018).

2. For further reading and statistics, see Michelle Alexander, *The New Jim Crow: Mass Incarceration in the Age of Colorblindness* (New York: New Press, 2020).

3. For further reading and statistics, see Marybeth Shinn and Jill Khadduri, *In the Midst of Plenty: Homelessness and What to Do about It* (Hoboken, NJ: Wiley Blackwell, 2020).

4. Barbara Brown Taylor, *Leaving Church: A Memoir of Faith* (New York: Harper Collins, 2006), 219.

5. See Walter Brueggemann, *Sabbath as Resistance: Saying No in a Culture of Now* (Louisville: Westminster John Knox, 2014).

Chapter 11: Another World

1. This camp and the events in this chapter are depicted in the documentary *Saint Cloud Hill* by the Moving Picture Boys (Indie Rights, 2019). For more information and for options to watch the documentary, visit http://saintcloudhill.com.

2. Mary Jones, *The Autobiography of Mother Jones* (New York: Prism Key, 2011), 32.

3. Arundhati Roy at the World Social Forum, Porto Alegre, 2003 (World Social Forum, 2015), https://www.youtube.com/watch?v=z6SS7l4UdB8.

4. Paulo Freire, *Pedagogy of the Oppressed*, trans. Myra B. Ramos (New York: Seabury, 1970), 128

DISCUSSION GUIDE

Chapter 1: Upstream

1. Krinks writes about the passage from Isaiah 58 burrowing and sprouting in her like a seed. Is there a passage, poem, or quote that has been significant in your life? If so, what is it and what resonates with you about it? What internal or external changes has it brought about in your life?

2. What did you take away from Alonzo and Clemmie's talk about homelessness? What stood out to you about them or what they said? How does this disrupt stereotypes about people experiencing homelessness?

3. Krinks writes about how she and the other student organizers felt pressured to cancel the rally and march. Have you ever been pressured by people in positions of authority to abandon a course of action that you felt was right? What was that like? How did you respond? What was the outcome?

4. Krinks writes about feeling as if her "page had turned" on the day of the rally. What significant experiences in your life have marked the end or beginning of a new chapter?

Chapter 2: Descent

1. In this chapter, Krinks talks about learning to see a city from below. If you were to look at your city or town from below, what and who would you see? What is your relationship to the "underside" of your city or town?

2. The experience of encountering the man in the camel-colored coat sitting outside the station stands out to Krinks. How have you responded when you see someone asking for money or help? What feelings arise for you? What options do you have other than turning away from the person as Krinks does? What does Krinks plan to do if she sees the man again?

3. Reading about Dorothy Day proves to be life changing for Krinks. After she reads Day's autobiography, she poses this question: "What would happen if I—if *we*—had the courage to live as if our deepest convictions were really true?" How would you respond to this question in your own life?

4. Later in this chapter, Krinks asks where she should go to find God and what religion is for. Where, or when, do you experience God or the sacredness and mystery of life most fully? If you are religious and/or spiritual, what purpose does your religion and/or spirituality play in your life?

Chapter 3: Broken Soil

1. Most of us have had times when we've felt broken or powerless. How did you get through these times? Who did you lean on for support? What did you learn about yourself, others, or the world during these times?

2. In this chapter, Krinks wrestles with going back and forth between places of extreme wealth and extreme poverty.

What is your relationship with wealth? What is your relationship with poverty? What do you think Krinks means when she says, "I was beginning to understand the poverty of wealth"?

3. After talking about the Great Recession, Krinks says, "Perhaps our system wasn't so much broken as it was working exactly how it was supposed to work, benefiting those at the top for whom it was created." Who seems to be "winning" in society today? Who seems to be losing? What could bring about more equity?

Chapter 4: Downhill

1. What rules in our society—spoken or unspoken, written or unwritten—keep us separated from people whose backgrounds differ from our own? What or who perpetuates these rules? What could happen if you—if we—were to break them?

2. In what ways have you seen organized religion perpetuate unjust systems and structures? In what ways have you seen organized religion *challenge* unjust systems and structures?

3. What stood out to you in "The Multitudes" section where Krinks talked about the foot clinic and meeting people like Kandy, Lily, Cathy, and Kentucky? What resonates with you in this quote from Parker Palmer: "Here's the deal. The human soul doesn't want to be advised or fixed or saved. It simply wants to be witnessed—to be seen, heard and companioned exactly as it is"?

4. How do the relational outreach and co-liberation models of engagement contrast with models of engagement that are more transactional and have clear distinctions between the givers and recipients of care?

Chapter 5: Burning Hearts

1. In this chapter, Krinks tells about her encounter with a man named Davie. Despite her best efforts to connect with him, what power imbalances still separated Krinks and her friends experiencing homelessness? Can someone who hasn't experienced homelessness truly understand what it's like to live without housing?

2. Krinks quotes theologian Mark Lewis Taylor, who says, "To embrace and love the executed God is to be in resistance to empire." What do you think Taylor means by this? If you agree with Taylor, what implications could this have for your life or the lives of people of faith?

3. During Holy Week on the Streets, Krinks and her group wrestled with a number of questions that arose as they read Scripture on the streets. How would you respond to these questions: How does our society encourage us to accumulate wealth and possessions? What are we hoarding that others could use?

4. Think of and describe a time that you had the experience of your heart "burning within you."

Chapter 6: Wilderness

1. This chapter chronicles a season of wilderness and burnout in Krinks's life. What season of wilderness stands out in your life, your experience? How did it impact you? How did you survive that season and what external support or internal strength helped you?

2. When Tent City residents temporarily relocated to land in Antioch after the flood, why do you think some Antioch residents and community leaders responded with such outrage? Was anyone "right" in this situation?

3. What resonates with you in the section where Krinks discusses Dr. McClure's pastoral care class, responsibility *to* vs. responsibility *for* people, and the question she posed to Krinks: "What are you running from?"

Chapter 7: Emergence

1. In this chapter, Krinks writes about her friend Ken and the healing and sense of meaning that he experienced as he was dying. What contributed to Ken's transformation? What could it mean to "discover healing through our wounds," as Krinks writes?
2. Krinks describes feeling compelled to participate in the Occupy Wall Street movement. Have you ever felt like you just had to get involved in something because of your convictions or commitments—like you were being pulled toward it and couldn't stay out of it? If so, what was it and what was that experience like? What compelled your action?
3. After her experience of being silenced at church, Krinks writes, "In other words, charity-oriented love is safe, but justice-oriented love is dangerous." What might she mean by this? What is so dangerous about "justice-oriented love"?

Chapter 8: Accompaniment

1. What are some of the examples of radical hospitality that Krinks witnessed from her friends on the streets? How do these acts upend some of the stereotypes about people experiencing homelessness in our society? What is Krinks learning about accompaniment through these friends?
2. Krinks describes accompaniment in this chapter and has mentioned it in previous chapters as well. What does

accompaniment entail and what does it look like for her in the context of the apartment complex run by the slumlord? Where is accompaniment present in your life right now?

3. Poet Rainer Maria Rilke writes, "Live the questions now." What questions are you currently living? Are they questions of vocation? Faith or doubt? Something else? How might "living the questions" differ from simply receiving immediate answers to these questions?

Chapter 9: Wick

1. When writing about the aftermath of Jimmy Fulmer's death, Krinks brings up the concepts of hot anger and cold anger. What is the difference between the two? Is there a time for both? Why or why not?

2. In this chapter, Krinks grapples with her calling to chaplaincy and ordained ministry. She also describes the doors that have been closed to her as a woman in the Church of Christ denomination. What closed doors, obstacles, and barriers have you faced? How have those barriers thwarted you? How have you found ways around, through, or over them?

3. Krinks also writes about how powerful her father's acceptance of her calling was for her. Who have you seen break cycles of judgment and exclusion in your life? What cycles of exclusion do you feel called to break in your relationships and community?

Chapter 10: Tending Wounds

1. In this chapter, Krinks quotes theologian and Nazi resister Dietrich Bonhoeffer, who says, "We are not to simply

bandage the wounds of victims beneath the wheels of injustice, we are to drive a spoke into the wheel itself." Think of an injustice you see in society. What are some of the ways you and your community could go beyond bandage solutions and work toward preventing the injuries and injustices in the first place?

2. The residents at Pick-a-Tree Village faced a host of barriers when it came to getting off the streets and finding healing and stability. What are some of the personal and systemic barriers they faced? What helped them overcome these barriers?

3. As this chapter progresses, Krinks not only tends the wounds of others but also feels her wounds being tended. Part of her healing is learning that her worth isn't tied up in what she does or accomplishes but in who she is. She begins to find a sense of wholeness as she practices Sabbath—a sacred day of rest. What wounds might you have that need to be tended? Where does it hurt? What is keeping you from feeling whole? What might a path to greater wholeness look like for you?

Chapter 11: Another World

1. Captain Chris believed that the camp at Fort Negley gave people "a place to get off the streets, to get sober, to be in nature, to turn things around. I've seen people get off drugs out here," he said, "people get into housing. And it's all because they had somewhere to start, people to care." How is it that a place with such few resources could become a place of such care and transformation? What does this tell you about Captain Chris's vision and resilience?

2. Where do Krinks and others "pray with their feet" in this chapter? What different forms of solidarity are shown

throughout? Where have you felt called to stand in greater solidarity with others and to pray with your feet?

3. If you were to believe that another world—a better world—was truly possible, what would that world look like? What would change? What are some small steps you could take to live into that world in the here and now?

Lindsey Krinks is cofounder of Open Table Nashville, an interfaith homeless outreach nonprofit. She received her master of theological studies degree from Vanderbilt University Divinity School and serves on its alumni council. She was ordained in 2013 and in 2018 became a fellow with the New Leaders Council, a national network for millennial leaders. She regularly speaks with student, church, and community groups across the country.

Printed in the United States
By Bookmasters